"Shklovsky is a disciple worthy of Sterne. He has appropriated the device of infinitely delayed events, of the digression helplessly promising to return to the point, and of disguising his superbly controlled art with a breezy nonchalance. But it is not really Sterne that Shklovsky sounds like: it is an intellectual and witty Hemingway."—Guy Davenport, *National Review*

PRAISE FOR *ZOO, OR LETTERS NOT ABOUT LOVE*

"The animals of the nearby zoo are symbols of his fellow émigrés, captured and far from home. Telephones and automobiles—relatively new inventions in 1922—appear and reappear as magical agents of good and evil. This quasi-novel is a bizarre and brilliant book."—Charles Simmons, *New York Times*

"*Zoo, or Letters Not about Love* is a work of gossip, allusion and esoteric reference, with devices—some typographical—which Shklovsky borrowed from Sterne, whom he much admired."
—John Bayley, *Listener*

PRAISE FOR
A SENTIMENTAL JOURNEY: MEMOIRS, 1917-1922

"This first-hand account, by a leading Formalist, of a society in turmoil owes much to Sterne—utterly unsentimental, detached, fragmentary, paradoxical, the memoirs tell of experiences at the front, in Persia and in St. Petersburg, philosophical asides jostling with vivid recollections, literary reference with political comment."—*Times Literary Supplement*

VIKTOR Shklovsky
KNIGHT'S MOVE

TRANSLATION AND INTRODUCTION
BY RICHARD SHELDON

DALKEY ARCHIVE PRESS
NORMAL · LONDON

First published by Helikon as *Khod Konia* in 1923
Russian text copyright © 1985 by Varvara Shklovskaya-Kordi
Translation rights into the English language are granted by FTM Agency, Ltd.,
    Russia
English translation copyright © 2005 by Richard Sheldon
Introduction copyright © 2005 by Richard Sheldon

First edition, 2005

Library of Congress Cataloging-in-Publication Data:

Shklovskii, Viktor Borisovich, 1893-1984
    [Khod konia. English]
    Knight's move / by Viktor Shklovsky ; translation by Richard Sheldon.—
1st Dalkey Archive ed.
        p. cm.
    ISBN 1-56478-385-5 (alk. paper)
    I. Sheldon, Richard (Richard Robert) II. Title.

    PG3476.S488K513 2005
    891.73'42—dc22

                                                    2004063481

Partially funded by a grant from the Illinois Arts Council, a state agency.

Dalkey Archive Press is a nonprofit organization located at Milner Library
(Illinois State University) and distributed in the UK by
Turnaround Publisher Services Ltd. (London).

www.dalkeyarchive.com

TABLE OF CONTENTS

TRANSLATOR'S INTRODUCTION

Trotsky's Objections

As a charter Futurist and Formalist, Shklovsky was accustomed to being omitted from Soviet reference books after 1930. After the death of Stalin in 1953, his literary criticism began to be published again. Finally, in 1969, a fairly comprehensive bibliography of his work appeared in the series *Russkie prozaiki*. Still, *Knight's Move* was not included. It seems that the book was ideologically tainted by its connection to Trotsky.

In the essay entitled "Ulya, Ulya Martians," Shklovsky put forward five propositions to demonstrate the independence of art from life. In his article "The Formalist School of Poetry and Marxism," Trotsky attacked Shklovsky's propositions and with heavy-handed sarcasm referred to Shklovsky as "a very capable high school boy who had a very evident and quite 'self-sufficient' intention to 'stick a pin into our teacher of literature, a noble pedant.'"

Trotsky treats Shklovsky's five propositions as separate assaults on various tenets of Marxism and then criticizes Shklovsky for repeating himself. In fact, the five propositions—the first general, the other four particular—are examples to put forward the proposition that art is independent of life.

Trotsky admits the similarities among plots of different cultures, but he attributes these similarities to borrowing and to the limited repertory of themes. The fact that novels of different societies show plot similarities suggests to Trotsky similarities in the societies.

As Victor Erlich points out, however, Trotsky overlooks Shklovsky's main point: not so much the similarity of themes as the similarity of compositional treatment, which indicated to Shklovsky the presence of general laws of plot composition.

Trotsky concluded his article with the statement that the word is the "phonetic shadow of the deed." In his book *Theory of Prose*, Shklovsky responded: "The word is not a shadow but a thing."

Apart from the problems with Trotsky, Shklovsky did not endear himself to the new regime by his skeptical remarks about Marxism and its determination to control art:

> The greatest misfortune of our time is that we are regulating art without knowing what it is.

> The greatest misfortune of Russian art is that it is not allowed to move organically, as the heart in the breast of a human being moves: it is being regulated like the movement of trains.

> Futurism was one of the purest achievements of human genius. It was a milestone, showing how much our understanding of the laws governing the freedom of creative work had increased. And it's impossible to shield the eye from that rustling tail of newspaper editorials that is now being attached to Futurism.

The forms of production relations are changing. Change in art is not the result of changes in daily life. They are the results of eternal petrification, the eternal passage of things from palpable perception to recognition.

Art has always been free of life. Its flag has never reflected the color of the flag that flies over the city fortress.

The title *Knight's Move* draws upon chess terminology, reinforced by a drawing of a knight moving across a chessboard. As Shklovsky explains in the first preface, the title has three meanings: 1) the conventions of art: the knight moves in an L-shaped manner because of such a convention; 2) the non-freedom of art: the knight moves in an L-shaped manner because other directions are forbidden to it; and 3) the plight of Shklovsky himself, referring to his escape from Russia in March of 1922. He says, "The path of the knight is not that of a coward. I'm no coward."

Within the articles Shklovsky uses the title twice as a reference point. In "Apropos of King Lear," he condemns the critics who write voluminously about Lear's madness. Viewing this madness as only a literary convention, Shklovsky draws a parallel between the knight and King Lear: "It would be interesting to find out what disease the knight has: you see, he always moves in an L-shaped manner."

In the epilogue, entitled "The Tsar's Kitchen," Shklovsky uses the title again. He precedes this reference with an anecdote about a tsar so rich that 3000 camels are required just to transport his kitchen equipment and staff. The tsar loses everything in a war except one pot. As he eats out of that pot, a dog comes along, catches itself on the handle and carries away the last vestige of the tsar's once-magnificent kitchen. The tsar laughs because one dog can now carry away the kitchen that 3000 camels once transported.

This anecdote illustrates the plight of Shklovsky, who lost all that he valued in leaving Russia. He follows this anecdote with a plea that he be allowed to return to Russia and then he invokes the title:

> Here is the end of the knight's move.
> *The knight turns his head and laughs.*

If the title provides one set of meaningful references, another is provided by a frame, which is put in place at the beginning of the book and closed at the end. The opening section consists of a piece called "Petersburg during the Blockade," which is a brilliant picture of the hardships that racked the city during the civil war when Petrograd was under siege and food and fuel were virtually unavailable. It was a dress rehearsal for the siege that the city was to undergo during World War II. Effectively using a detached narrative point of view, Shklovsky conveys all the horror of those days in the most matter-of-fact terms. A typical sentence: "It's hard to be a horse in Petersburg." This approach to the suffering city reflects Shklovsky's belief that material innately sensational should be treated with restraint.

All the elements of the book discussed so far are part of the frame. It encloses a core of thirty-six articles, all written during the civil war, all published in the tiny theater journal *The Life of Art* between 1919 and 1921.

These are essentially the dates of the period known as War Communism, when the victorious Bolsheviks began to implement their policies, concentrating on the nationalization of industry and the control of agriculture. The failure of these policies soon led to strikes and peasant revolts, culminating in the Kronstadt Uprising in March 1921, when the sailors stationed there rose up, demanding more freedom. The government responded by shooting or imprisoning more than 14,000 of the sailors. At that point Lenin saw that the Party was not strong enough yet to impose its programs so he ordered a reversal of policy, which became known as the New Economic Policy (NEP) and which was to last until the end of the decade.

In *Knight's Move*, then, we have a detailed account of Russian society as it was developing between the revolution and NEP. Shklovsky was very nervous about the new government's intentions with regard to the arts. He was right to be worried, but the new government had to postpone implementation of its programs, which made possible the brilliant achievements in the arts during the twenties. Taking advantage of this more relaxed period, Shklovsky was allowed to return to the Soviet Union in March 1923.

This book explores the nature of art, defends the independence of art and demonstrates the new formalist criticism.

The Need for a New Kind of Theater

In the heated discussions about the direction the theater should take after the revolution, Anatoly Lunacharsky favored a revival of all the classics in order to acquaint the masses with the cultural landmarks of the past. Shklovsky opposed this plan. True to his Futurist allegiance, with its wholesale rejection of the art of the past, Shklovsky felt that the revolutionary theater should not rely on old favorites no longer vital enough to elicit perception. He called for a boycott on the plays of the following authors: Goethe, Chekhov, Shakespeare, Sophocles, Rostand, Merezhkovsky and Ostrovsky. Instead, he advocated Marlow's *Faust* (rather than Goethe's), the plays of Khlebnikov and Blok, and Mayakovsky's *Mystery-Bouffe*.

In Mayakovsky's play, Shklovsky found a worthy model for a revolutionary theater. Although he considered the ending weak, he admired the dialogue. Referring to Meyerhold's production in the fall of 1918, Shklovsky protested that after a few performances, it had been taken out of production "like a hostile flag traitorously raised over the fortress, then ripped down." Shklovsky reviewed Meyerhold's new production in May 1921, with Mayakovsky's revised text and stage sets by Malevich, and found the use of extraliterary material especially striking—the projection of pictures of the fortress of Peter and Paul.

In his formal analysis of *King Lear*, Shklovsky dismisses as irrelevant all the discussions of the play as a reflection of reality. He views the play as a verbal construct which takes the pun as its material. He notes that Shakespeare uses obvious conventions and makes no attempts to motivate his devices, as the numerous non-recognition scenes and clumsy denouements show. The daughters are pure conventions—card women, with Cordelia as the trump:

> The content of *King Lear,* in my opinion, I repeat, is not the tragedy of a father, but a series of situations,

a series of witticisms, a series of devices organized in such a way that they create, by their interrelations, new stylistic devices . . . . *King Lear* is a stylistic phenomenon.

During the years covered by Shklovsky's articles, circus acts were frequently interpolated into the texts of plays for various special effects. Shklovsky applied his analytic techniques to the circus. He points out that circus performers—trapeze artists, lion tamers, weight lifters—all engage in acts which require overcoming obstacles. Drawing upon his theoretical observations about impeded form in literature, Shklovsky concludes that the fundamental device of the circus is impediment, which delays the successful completion of each act and which generates suspense.

Vsevolod Meyerhold revolutionized the Russian theater during the first decades of the twentieth century. Nikolai Gorchakov summarized the innovations Meyerhold introduced and developed:

The return to forms used by folk theater in the past, the stubborn struggle with the illusions of the scenic box, the forcible removal of its finery, the unveiling of the "kitchen," that is, the technical work that goes into a production, the baring of the stage, the advancing of the proscenium, the removal of the curtain and the footlights, the filling up of the orchestra pit, the construction of steps and gangways to the auditorium and the transferral of actors to it, the compulsory participation of the audience in the acts, and the hundreds of Meyerhold's other clever devices would galvanize the audience of the intimate theater and aim at making it the fourth creator of the theater.

In particular, Meyerhold's experimentation with the interpolation of circus acts and topical scenes into a basic text, as well as his use of devices of folk theater, proved influential. Sergei Radlov used these techniques in the productions of his Folk Comedy Theater in Petrograd from 1919 to 1922; Yury Annenkov used them in his experimental production of Tolstoy's *The First Distiller* at the Hermitage Theater in 1919. The innovations and concepts of Meyerhold and his disciples regarding the theater have much in common with Shklovsky's ideas about literature. Both valued experimentation; both insisted on innovation; both liked to bare to the audience the armature of the work of art—the manipulations of the author, the techniques by which the work is assembled. In his article entitled "Psychological Footlights," Shklovsky praises the "flicker effect" in literature and in the theater—the techniques by which an author or director creates an illusion of reality, then deliberately shatters that illusion.

Shklovsky, however, opposed the main experimental trends of an extremely avant-garde period of Russian theater. In 1920, Meyerhold mounted a sensational new production of Emile Verhaeren's *Les aubes*. Into the original text of the play, Meyerhold interpolated scenes from the Russian civil war, which was still happening. He set the whole production against a Futuristic background of "cubes, ropes, mobiles, golden circles, triangles of shiny metal."

This production was scornfully rejected by Shklovsky. He objected both to the play and to Meyerhold's inventions. In Shklovsky's opinion, Meyerhold had failed to exploit the "flicker effect." By modernizing the basic text to conform to the interpolations, he had smoothed over the transitions between them and lost the sharp contrasts that could have been obtained between the basic text and the topical interpolations.

At first glance, it seems surprising that Shklovsky would oppose the theater of Meyerhold with its vivid effects and its conception of acting as the application of certain techniques to derive a certain effect. Yet a closer look at Meyerhold's theories makes Shklovsky's reasons for disapproval clear.

According to Meyerhold's "theory of biomechanics," certain gestures elicit from the spectator certain emotions. The actor merely learns a set of body movements and manipulates them according to the effect desired. "All," he said, "is the mute eloquence of the body. The word is but an embroidery on the canvas of movement." Shklovsky had categorically rejected Trotsky's view of the word as a shadow and he could also not accept Meyerhold's view of the word as an embroidery. The word is a thing.

In this area, two of his value judgments conflict: his predilection for innovation and striking effects clashes with his reverence for the word. To Shklovsky the techniques of Meyerhold and the acrobatic theater sacrificed the word to striking visual effects. Only in Mayakovsky's

Mystery-Bouffe did Shklovsky find a real orientation to the word.

The Need for a New Kind of Painting and Sculpture

In painting, as in literature and theater, Shklovsky saw the fundamental problem as the manipulation of devices. The painter does not attempt to copy reality: he uses reality as material for the creation of "self-valuable (artistic) things."

To support this contention, Shklovsky discusses the mathematical formulas by which the painter calculates perspective and chiaroscuro. The artist uses set conventions to make a product of independent significance from nature.

Shklovsky strongly opposed painting and sculpture that slavishly copy reality and use hackneyed techniques, as he unequivocally showed in his scathing denunciation of Blokh's statue "The Great Metal Worker." Yet he did not wholeheartedly endorse the abstract art of the Suprematists.

In this instance, as in the case of Meyerhold and his experimental theater, one would have expected Shklovsky to approve the daring artistic experiments of the Suprematists. This school was first proclaimed by Kazimir Malevich (1878-1935) at an exhibition in Petrograd called "0.10. The Last Futurist Painting Exhibition," held in December 1915. In his spirited manifesto, Malevich argued for the "nullity of forms" and an art that spurned the "circle of things."

Malevich developed this style of painting out of the stage sets that he designed for the production of Kruchenykh's

Futurist opera, *Victory over the Sun*, also produced in December 1915. By using geometric elements as his basic material, Malevich created the first school of abstract painting in Russia.

In his assessment of the work of the Suprematists, Shklovsky was once again forced to choose between competing concepts of his own poetics. The paintings of the Suprematists "bared the device" and certainly elicited renewed peception of the painting. Yet their work fell short in what Shklovsky considered to be the very purpose of renewed perception: to thrust a recognizable object into relief. The key sentence that explains his opposition to the colored planes of the Suprematists is the following: "When we see an object, perception of the form occurs only when we recognize the object, recognize what it is."

In the work of Vladimir Tatlin (1885-1953), founder of the school of Constructivism, Shklovsky found more occasion for enthusiasm. Tatlin hated the abstract paintings of Malevich and, after a scandalous fistfight with him at the aforementioned exhibition "0.10," broke completely with Malevich and continued working out his Constructivist style. Tatlin experimented with collages of various materials; he sought to incorporate space into his constructions with the slogan: Real materials in real space.

In December 1920, Tatlin exhibited a model for an exciting spiral tower made of iron. This leaning tower, planned to be twice the height of the Empire State Building, was to support a huge glass cylinder, a glass cone and a glass cube. The cylinder, designed for meetings and conferences, would revolve on its axis once a year; the cone, designed for executive activities, would revolve once a month; the topmost cube, designed as an information center, once a day.

Shklovsky admired this daring design for its modern materials and its use of identifiable shapes in a new way. He gave this design his unqualified approval: "This is the first time that iron has stood on end and sought its artistic formula." Not surprisingly, this remarkable tower, called "To the Third International," was never built.

Fedin's Objections

In 1922, Konstantin Fedin, a member of the Serapion Brothers like Nitkitin and Lunts, published a clever parody of Shklovsky's *Knight's Move*, which Fedin had evidently seen in manuscript form. He called his piece *"Melok na shube"* (Chalk on the Fur Coat) and he published it in August 1921 in *The Life of Art*, the same journal where Shklovsky was publishing the individual pieces of *Knight's Move*.

With tongue in cheek, Fedin reproaches Shklovsky for the conservatism of his form. After all, why place the second preface after the first one . . . and why discuss the old theater before the new one? Since Shklovsky had helped the reader along by indicating where the middle of the book was, why not indicate where 5/8 of the book ended and where the 6th began?

Then Fedin mentions Dostoevsky and Gogol, whose work affects the reader so strongly. If they had bared their devices, Fedin suggests, this would all be changed—since they would have no readers. Fedin admits to a feeling of guilt because, he confesses, he has no idea where the middle of *Dead Souls* is to be found. What's worse, he admits, is that he has felt all these years that what matters in a writer is not literary devices but inspiration and creativity.

From these playful remarks, Fedin draws serious conclusions. He recognizes the importance of the Formalists' work, but feels that things have gotten out of hand. He expresses a distaste for all the studios where people learn to be creative writers and he wonders how Gogol, Tolstoy, Gorky, Leskov and Shchedrin ever managed without the valuable insights of the Formalists.

Fedin imagines that Shklovsky organized *Khod konya* according to certain principles and then couldn't resist showing how the book was made. Explaining the title of his article, Fedin comments that the chalk marks a tailor makes in fitting a fur coat are useful only to the tailor. In concluding, Fedin says that when he showed the article to Shklovsky, the latter remarked, "Good! Now we can write about how your feuilleton was made."

"He's right . . . He's right . . ."

Shklovsky ends his book with a reference to the title, citing the last line: "The knight turns his head and laughs," meaning what? The sentence pointing to chess as the primary reference does not exhaust all the possibilities. The word *kon'* means not only 'knight' but also 'horse' or 'steed.' Shklovsky's final sentence, then, bears the insignia of the Futurists—a laughing horse.

Richard Sheldon
1 October 2004

KNIGHT'S MOVE

K N I G H T ' S   M O V E

First Preface

This book is called *Knight's Move*. The knight moves in
an L-shaped manner, like this:

There are many reasons for the strangeness of the
knight's move, the main one being the conventionality of
art, about which I am writing.

The second reason lies in the fact that the knight is not
free—it moves in an L-shaped manner because it is forbidden to take the straight road.

The articles and feuilletons included in this book were
all published in Russia from 1919 through 1921.

They were published in the tiny theater newspaper called *The Life of Art*. That newspaper itself was a knight's move.

I'm writing for those Russians living abroad.

Some say——in Russia people are dying in the street; in Russia people are eating, or are capable of eating, human flesh . . .

Others say——in Russia the universities are functioning; in Russia the theaters are full.

You choose for yourself what to believe.

But why choose? It's all true.

——In Russia there is something else.

——In Russia everything is so contradictory that we have all become witty in spite of ourselves.

I've left these newspaper articles as they were written. Very little has been added.

One more word——don't think that the knight's move is the coward's move.

I'm no coward.

Our tortuous road is the road of the brave, but what are we to do if we see with our own two eyes more than honest pawns and dutiful kings.

B U N D L E

Second Preface

Two members of my workshop came to see me: Lev Lunts and Nikolai Nikitin.

They said to me: "Tell us something about art because we are members of your workshop."

And I replied: "I will tell you something like an excerpt from the Hitopadesa—a story within a story. It will be interesting as an example of Indian poetics. I care about your education, because you are members of my workshop."

They said, "Fine."

"In a certain kingdom there lived a well-to-do peasant (*posrednik*). In the fall he harvested grain from the field, ground it and swore. At that moment there came an old man, who said to him:

—Why are you swearing? You are befouling the clean air. Isn't it enough that you can swear in your hut?

And the peasant replied:

—Who wouldn't swear? The harvest was bad. Once again Nicholas the Wonderworker made a mess of things. When fair weather was needed, he sent rain; when sun was needed, he sent frost.

But actually the old man was none other than Nicholas the Wonderworker himself.

Nicholas the Wonderworker took offense and said to him:

—Well, if my way of making the weather doesn't suit you, here's a mandate for you: make the weather yourself.

The peasant was overjoyed. He began to organize the weather himself.

But when fall came and he harvested the grain, the harvest was bad, very bad.

He threshed the grain and he swore. He swore so vigorously that horses passing by on the road averted their snouts.

Along came Nicholas the Wonderworker. He laughed:

—How was the harvest?

The peasant swore so vigorously that the fleeting cloudlets gasped.

—You call that a harvest?

—Tell me, then, how you made the weather.

The peasant told everything in a series of paragraphs.

The Wonderworker laughed.

—You did have wind?

—Why would I want wind? It only mixes up the grain.

—Wind is essential. Without wind neither rye nor wheat is pollinated. I assume, then, that there was no storm.

—No.

—But a storm is essential.

At that point the peasant had a thought, which he passed on to the Wonderworker:

—You know, maybe you should make the weather yourself.

And the Wonderworker said to him:

—Actually, you have acted the way people in Italy act when they subsequently become idiots.

—And how do people in Italy act when they subsequently become idiots?—asked the peasant.

—In Italy or Japan there lived people who began to notice without any help, or else others after them noticed, that they were growing more stupid by the day, and in summer three hours ahead of time. They asked doctors. The doctors racked their brains and came up with the following guess: These Japanese or Italian people have been eating husked rice. The part which is necessary to the brain is in the rice, but only in its husk. And then the doctors said:

—Don't go around inventing food without taking into account every eventuality, but if the people who became idiots because they failed to eat husks are like the peasant who forgot about the wind, then the man who would have liked to take everything into account would be like the Indian folk tale about the millipede.

—And what is this tale about the millipede, asked the people who had become idiots.

The doctors said:

—There was once a millipede and it had exactly a thousand legs, if not fewer, and it ran swiftly, so the turtle envied it.

Then the turtle said to the millipede:

—How wise you are! And how is it that you can guess and how is it that you have the quick-wittedness to know how to arrange your leg number 978 when you put forward leg number 5?

At first, the millipede was overcome with joy and pride, but then he really started to think about the location of each of his legs; he introduced centralization, red tape and bureaucracy and was incapable of moving a single leg.

Then it said:

—Viktor Shklovsky was right when he said that the greatest misfortune of our time is that the government is regulating art without knowing what it is. The greatest misfortune of Russian art is that we discard it like a husk of rice. And by the way, art in general is not one of the methods of propaganda, it is like vitamins, which should be contained in food in addition to proteins and fats. Vitamins are neither protein nor fat, but the life of the organism is impossible without them.

The greatest misfortune of Russian art is that it is not allowed to move organically, as the heart moves in a man's chest: it is being regulated like the movement of trains.

The millipede said:

—Citizens and comrades, look at me and you will see what excessive regulation leads to! Comrades of the revolution, comrades of the war, leave art alone, not in its own name but in the name of the fact that it's impossible to regulate the unknown!

—Well, so what?—asked the members of my workshop.

—Now you must say something in order to close the frame, which is traditional in Indian poetics—I replied.

—We have squandered our youth—said Lev Lunts and Nikolai Nikitin as they left.

They are extremely capable people. Lunts has written a play called *The Apes Are Coming*; Nikitin has written a short story called "The Stake."

SETTING THE FRAME

Petersburg During the Blockade

What struck me in Moscow was the abundance of crows. The first time they frightened me was on the Square Okhotny Ryad. On the reddish-blue horseflesh brought to some food stall sat the black crows with their grayish-blue breasts. The horseflesh and the crows went well together. The crows matched the terrible, flayed horses' heads. A horse's carcass is not attractive. No one threatened the crows and they threatened no one, but calmly walked about on the strong meat-like rooks in a plowed field.

It was spring. The weather was turning warm. I was walking home to Ostozhenka, where I was staying. In the air some sort of "crow festival" was taking place. The crows were flying over the Cathedral of Christ the Savior in a spiral as if they were trying to surround Moscow. They were flying in formation and I felt like an infantryman cut off by a charge of the cavalry.

Some crows (it seemed like many) swirled around the cupola of the cathedral like flies. It made the cupola look dirty. They cawed and screeched and made an awful racket as they wheeled in the air over the city, which was half-immersed in dirty snow. They formed ranks, shifting constantly in the air. Then several of the crow battalions landed on a building with eleven chimneys just in front of the cathedral. The roof turned black. I don't know what the crows were up to, but they were certainly up to something. Perhaps it was just a demonstration.

At night in Moscow the crows roost in the trees along Prechistensky Boulevard, not far from the Arbat. The trees are so laden with crows that it seems as if the leaves, instead of falling from the branches in autumn, merely turned black.

Now the crows in Petersburg are not visible.

Petersburg lives and dies simply, without histrionics.

I want to write about it. How else will people know how we starved, how many victims the revolution cost, what efforts each step of the revolution took.

Who will be able to recall the meaning of newspaper accounts and shed light on the everyday life of a great city at the end of the Petersburg period and at the beginning of a history as yet unknown?

I am writing in March, at the beginning of spring, 1920. Much has already transpired. The hardest part already seems like a memory. I'm even writing with a full stomach, but I remember the hunger, the hunger that stands watch over us on all sides.

There are few streetcars in Petersburg, but those few are functioning. They go mainly to the outskirts. The cars are full to the brim. To the rear of the cars, especially at the train stations, children with sleds attached themselves, as did children on ice skates—sometimes whole rows of them.

Streetcars carry the mail. Nowadays, using makeshift platforms attached to streetcars, people haul dirt and trash from temporary dumps arranged on various streets.

One of them is to be found on the corner of Nevsky and Liteiny.

Petersburg is dirty because it is very tired. You might wonder why it should be dirty. There are not many people: about 700,000. Scraps of paper and wood chips—everything is burned in little homemade stoves, which are called "bourgeoiskis." Petersburg produces hardly any litter. It's too destitute to generate litter. Petersburg is dirty (in moderation and less so than Moscow). Petersburg is dirty and, at the same time, tidy, like a horribly weak, sick man who lies there and soils himself.

During the winter almost all the toilets froze. That was somewhat worse than the hunger. Right, first the water froze. It was impossible to wash oneself. In the Talmud it is said that when there is not enough water for drinking and for ablutions, then it is better not to drink but to wash oneself. But we didn't wash. The toilets froze. How that happened, history will tell. The revolution and the blockade, with the blow it delivered on the outside, destroyed the transportation system. There was no firewood. The water froze.

All of us, almost the entire city, carried water up and human waste down. Up and down we carried buckets every day. How hard it was to live without a toilet. A professor friend and I were walking down the street numb with the cold when he said to me with such grief: "You know, I envy the dogs. At least they don't have to be ashamed."

The city soiled itself in courtyards, under gates, almost on rooftops. This looked bad and sometimes sort of mischievous. Some individuals would flaunt their indignation with feces.

I'm writing about a terrible year and about a city during the blockade. Ezekiel and Jeremiah cooked cakes on dung in order to show the inhabitants of Jerusalem what would happen to them in case of a siege.

In Petersburg every day cakes were cooked on human feces; on holidays horse manure was used.

People urinated a lot that year—shamelessly, more shamelessly than I can describe—in broad daylight right on Nevsky, wherever. They urinated without unhitching themselves from their sledges, without taking off the yoke, without removing the rope by which these sledges are pulled.

Here was defeat mingled with hopelessness. In order to stay alive, you had to fight, to fight every single day. For each degree of warmth you had to stand in line. For cleanliness you had to scrub your hands with ashes.

Then the louse fell upon the city. Lice attack out of grief.

Now for a few words about the temperature.

Those of us living from day to day went into the winter without any firewood. To get it with coupons was very difficult. You had to endure standing in two cold and hostile lines and then there wasn't enough wood even for the kitchens.

What did we burn? A few of the surviving bourgeoisie went into business for themselves selling a sugar substitute mixed with some other mysterious ingredient. They heated with firewood. We heated with everything. I burned my furniture, my sculptor's stand, bookcases and books, books beyond calculation and measure. If my arms and legs had been made of wood, I would have burned them and appeared in the spring without limbs.

One friend of mine burned nothing but books. His wife sat by the smoky iron stove and kept shoving into it journal after journal. In other parts of town people burned doors and furniture from other people's apartments. It was a festival of conflagration. Wooden buildings were dismantled and burned. Big buildings devoured small ones. In the rows of houses appeared deep gaps, where separate buildings stuck out like teeth. People carried out the demolition weakly and ineptly. They would forget to remove chimneys. They would break glass. They would dismantle one wall instead of tearing the house down starting from the top as one unreels a spool of thread. Artificial ruins made their appearance. The city slowly began to transform itself into an engraving by Piranesi.

But the frost penetrated the walls of the houses, freezing them to the wallpaper. People slept in their overcoats and their galoshes. Everyone congregated in the kitchen. In the abandoned rooms stalactites appeared. People huddled together in the deserted city as close as in a box of toys. Priests in their churches conducted the liturgy in gloves and chasubles worn over fur coats. Sick school children all froze. The Arctic Circle became a reality. It passed through the city somewhere around Nevsky. It was then that the graves of old houses opened. On Nevsky people took down and burned the scaffolding on the buildings being reconstructed and those buildings appeared once again as old dead walls.

And the buildings being constructed were denied the right to be born; their scaffolding was also taken down.

Then, too, I forgot to say that men were almost completely impotent and women ceased to have their periods.

13

That didn't happen right away. Wave after wave of hunger first weakened, then lashed everyone as it dragged them under.

When the pressure doesn't exceed the usual norms, objects change their form in a variety of ways, but when the pressure is enormous, it obliterates the differences between a hardness of straw and a hardness of iron. It all takes a single shape.

In Petersburg the pressure was extreme. The inhabitants of Petersburg had but one fate. Everything was experienced as a series of epidemics. There were the months of rubber heels when all the shops had white signs trimmed in blue and red. All the shops were selling sheets of rubber. There were the months of antique shops when everyone was selling everything in various shops with strange names, such as "Po-ko-ko." There was the month of falling horses when every day on every street weakened horses, unable to get up, jerked convulsively on the pavement. There was the month when there was nothing to be found in the shops except little packets of saccharine.

There was the month when everybody ate only cabbage. That was in the fall, when Yudenich was attacking. There was the month when everyone was eating potato peels and, before that everyone had been eating cocoa butter.

Petersburg moved like a herd. It began to hurl itself in various directions. There were no faces: they had been wiped out. But now let me say a few words about horses. It's hard to be a horse in Petersburg. When a horse is not fed, it falls on the stones and jerks. It keeps jerking, trying desperately without horseshoes to gain a foothold on the bare, round—invariably round—cobblestones. We felt sorry for our horses. Whenever a horse fell, people came running from all directions, but not on the sidewalks—there were no sidewalks. Everyone walked down the middle of the street and tried with all their strength to get the horse on its feet, not even fearing mange.

But a fallen horse can hardly ever be raised. It falls and it lies there. People put some hay by its head. On the first day the horse chews the hay, then it lies motionless next to it. It can no longer raise its head. Then the dogs come.

Dogs don't tear at a dead horse. They're incompetent, Petersburg dogs. They have lost the art of tearing meat.

At first people furtively cut chunks off the carcass. Then the joyful dogs bit into the exposed meat. Sometimes you ran across a horse's tail or a piece of horse where you didn't remember seeing the corpse of a horse. And if you haul a dead horse to a rendering plant, the head hangs over the side of the wagon and the enfeebled lips dangle and seem to be emitting a discharge.

Horse bones (spine and ribs) lay all winter at the end of Yamskaya Street, reminding me of the caravan routes. There the bones were even more numerous.

Life was harder for cats. I never saw them on the corpses, but one time as I was going to visit an acquaintance, I saw a cat at his door. It was just standing there, waiting. It looked very thin but dignified. I don't know what its relations were with the house by whose door it was standing. When I left, after staying no longer than an hour, the cat was lying on its side, peaceful but dead.

Cats die peacefully in Petersburg.

Now about dogs. I will not attempt to describe a dog's life. I'm not attentive enough for that. I remember only the beggar dogs. One stood at the corner of Simeopovsky and Mokhovaya Street. Another on Panteleleimonovsky by the church. A third on the corner of Grechesky and Basseinaya. Two fox terriers and one poodle (the poodle was on Basseinaya). They stood on their hind legs and begged, or they stood and simply barked. People went up to them and brought them food. They stood there for months, then disappeared.

Let's return to people. How hard it was to pull sledges with firewood or with furniture, especially when the snow had melted or the runners were not sheathed. Or to thrash around on the slippery ice and, falling, dream about strong, persistent hoofs with spiked shoes.

I will not forget the grief of squeaky runners.

People died simply and frequently. After all, I'm speaking about the general situation. In the commissary of the House of Writers, where it smelled of bad food, and where people who had been frozen out of their apartments sat along the walls and dreamed—people who were already consigned by the frost and darkness to chaos. In the darkness on the wall there already hung one, two or three families of the dead. Someone called it the dish of the week.

A man dies. He has to be buried. A hard frost freezes the street. The family calls an acquaintance or a relative; they get a coffin; maybe they rent one. They go to the cemetery.

I witnessed the following scene. The family is dragging a man. The children are small, very small. They push and cry. What happened at the cemetery I don't know. I'm too inattentive.

The corpses were hauled from the hospitals in coffins and stacked, with three on the bottom crosswise, then two going the other way or in mattress bags. There was no one to straighten out the corpses. They were buried as they were—contorted.

Hunger. We got used to living with hunger like a lame man with his lameness.

The morning began with hunger and boiled water. That was followed after dinner by bickering in the family over food. There was hunger at night. We starved submissively. The hungry spoke with the hungry about hunger. It was hard to watch someone eating. I saw one man eating a dried fish while another, who had come to pay him a visit, furtively took the bones and the fishheads from the edge of the plate and ate them on the spot. Both men pretended that this was nothing at all, that this was the way it had always been done. Food ceased to be filling. When there was food, people ate it but without ever getting full.

We ate strange things: frozen potatoes, rotten turnips and herring with the tails and heads cut off so that they didn't smell so bad. We cooked them in drying oil. We ate lead salt, oats with their husks and horsemeat already soft from decay. There was little bread to be had. At first it was awful, laced with straw and reminiscent of those brickets made of stalks. Then the bread got better and became soft. We ate it, deliberately.

Hunger and jaundice. We were immersed in hunger like a fish in water, like birds in the air.

One of my acquaintances got married to a cook in a communist commissary, another to a chauffeur who trafficked in stolen kerosene. He felt sorry for her and gave her some bread and some laced boots that went all the way to the knee. If there had been a slave market at which one could have sold oneself for bread, it would have done more business than all those shops selling saccharine.

All around the city lay the village. Before, the city drew everything from the village, and grew, swelled and became more beautiful. Now the city is melting into the village like soap in water. People have left. They have remembered the land. The shopkeeper and the barber have returned to the village. The skilled worker has left the factory. Anyone else who could has also crawled out.

Then the village stripped the city, bartering drapes for bread and potatoes, dishes for fat. The bagman was strong and serious, master of his land and owner of his own skin. With his bag he took everything from the city: gold, gramophones, icons, clothes—everything, it seems, except books.

Here's how we were dressed. A woman's outfit, brought to her by a black marketeer, was like this: felt boots, a sweater, a warm cap and a sealskin coat, but I don't really remember what our women wore. I didn't look at them. It was too pathetic. We dressed like Eskimoes. Those who could get their hands on them wore felt boots, a sheepskin coat and a regular coat cinched with a belt. The head was wrapped in scarfs. We wore soldiers' pants tucked into our boots. But, mainly we were wearing everything old. I remember some remnants of a military uniform. We wore cloth slippers. We wound our legs with rags or we wore galoshes on the bare leg or on the leg wrapped in rags. But many by some sort of miracle didn't die. The old supplies of the city were dwindling but hadn't completely run out.

People put homemade mittens on their hands. When you put a mitten on the left hand, it seemed as if it were on the right; when you put a mitten on the right hand, it seemed to be for the left.

We washed rarely, and only the hardiest at that.

At times it seemed that we could not hold out any longer. Everyone would freeze to death at night in the apartments. Wounds were so deep. And wounds without fat don't heal. A scratch gets infected. Everyone's hands were swathed in very dirty rags. It was impossible to heal and to regain one's health. As for the great city, it continued to live.

It lived by its city soul, the soul of many, as a pile of coal smolders under the rain. (O darkness and the soot of the little nightlight and the waiting for the light!) We left our dark apartments to gather at the theaters. We looked at the stage. Hungry actors played their parts, hungry writers wrote, scholars did their work.

We gathered and we sat in our coats by the stove, where books were burning. There were wounds on our legs. From a lack of fat, blood vessels burst. And we talked about rhythm, about verbal form and, now and then, about spring, which we had little hope of seeing.

So lived many, including old professors in their typhus-ridden apartments. It seemed that we worked not by the head but by the spinal cord. The Neva flowed beneath the ice; it flowed and we worked.

I understand those who fought at the approach to Petrograd and repelled the enemy. The city, exhausted to the bone, was warm with the heat of a feverish patient. The city was sick with a great sickness—revolution. Though dying, Petersburg never became provincial. Those going from it were melting from its heat. Few knew that they were burning, but many burned.

The old life has ended and we are in the desert. I don't know where I'm going, but I don't want to go back. I have learned to value what has happened. The old family has died. We have ceased to love our things. We have forgotten our old places. It would be too hard to go back.

The city is empty. The streets have become so much wider that it's as though they had washed away the shores. But the city is still alive and it is burning either like a fire or like a wound on the body of rural Russia. This is the red fire of revolution—all that is left of the city in Russia.

REGARDING ART AND REVOLUTION[*]

"Ullya, Ullya, Martians"
(*from* The Trumpet of the Martians)

The words that I'm writing now are written with a feeling of great friendship for the people with whom I'm arguing.

But the mistakes now being made are so clear to me and will be so damaging to art that I cannot keep silent.

The most serious mistake of contemporary writers about art is, in my opinion, their tendency to equate the social revolution with the revolution in the arts.

The "Scythians," the "Futurist-Communists," the "Proletkult"—they all clamor incessantly for a new art that will correspond to the new-class ideology. The second premise is commonplace: Our art is new when it expresses the revolutionary will of the new-class and the new-world view. The proofs cited for that are usually incredibly naïve:

The "proletkult" usually shows its correspondence to the given moment by arguing that the parents of the poets were themselves proletarians. The "Scythians" are a purely literary device of the "folk language" in poetry, called forth by blending the old literary language with the city

---

[*]Written apropos of the Futurists' decision to "accept leadership positions in art under the aegis of the National Commissarat of Education (Narkompros)."

dialect and tracing its history from Leskov via Remizov. This establishes language as a sign of back-to-the-soil of its writers, while the Futurists cite proofs of its organic hostility to the capitalist form of government by means of that hostility which the bourgeoisie has fed us since the days of our appearance on earth.

The proofs are not abundant. A weak foundation to support a bid for a berth in the history of social revolution—for a berth which we may need no more than sunlight needs an apartment with three rooms and a bath on Nevsky Prospekt.

All these proofs have one thing in common: All the authors suppose that new forms of daily life create new forms of art; that is to say, they consider that art is one of the functions of life.

The result is as follows: let us suppose that the facts of life are a row of numbers; then the phenomena of art will appear as logarithms of their numbers.

But actually we Futurists have entered the fray under a new banner: *New form gives birth to new content.* We have emancipated art from daily life, which plays in creative work only the role of fleshing out forms and may, perhaps even be driven out altogether, as Khlebnikov and Kruchenykh did when they wanted to flesh out Guillot's dictum that "poetry is the distance between rhymes." They fleshed it out with free spots of meaningless sound. But the Futurists were merely acknowledging the work of centuries. Art has always been free of life. Its flag has never reflected the color of the flag that flies over the city fortress.

Consider the following propositions:

(1) If daily life and production relations influenced art, is it not true that plots would be bound to their place of origin? But actually plots are homeless.

(2) If daily life were expressed in novellas, then European scholarship would not be tying itself in knots to find out where—in Egypt, India or Persia—and when were created the novellas that constitute *The Arabian Nights*.

(3) If class aspects were deposited in art, would it really be possible that the Russian folk tales about the landlord would be the same as the folk tales about the village priest?

(4) If ethnographic features were deposited in art, the folk tales about foreigners would not be reversible and would not be told by any given people about their neighbors.

(5) If art were so flexible that one could use it to illustrate changes in the conditions of everyday life, then the plot of abduction—which, as we see in the words of the slave in Menander's comedy, was by then already a purely literary tradition—would not have survived to Ostrovsky's day and would not have fleshed out literature like ants in a forest.

New forms appear in art in order to replace old forms which have ceased to be artistic.

It was Tolstoy who said that it was wrong to write using the forms of Gogol and Pushkin because those forms had already been discovered.

It was Aleksandr Veselovsky who set the stage for a free history of literary form.

And to think that we Futurists have connected our creative work to the Third International!

Comrades, this is the surrender of all positions! This is Belinsky-Vengerov and *The History of the Russian Intelligentsia*!

Futurism was one of the purest achievements of human genius.

It was a milestone, showing how much our understanding of the laws governing the freedom of creative work had increased. And it's impossible to shield the eye from that rustling tail of newspaper editorials that is now being attached to Futurism.

Pounding Nails with a Samovar

If you take hold of a samovar by its stubby legs, you can use it to pound nails, but that is not its primary function.

I saw war. With my own hands I stoked stoves with pieces of a piano in Stanislavov and made bonfires out of rugs and fed the flames with vegetable oil while trapped in the mountains of Kurdistan. Right now I'm stoking a stove with books. I know the laws of war and I understand that in its own way it reorganizes things, such as reducing a man to 180 pounds of human flesh, or using a rug as surrogate for a fuse.

But it's wrong to view a samovar with an eye to making it pound nails more easily or to write books so that they will make a hotter fire.

War—privation—reorganizes things in its own way, which is terrible but honest. However, to change the meaning of things, to bore through a door with a spoon, to shave oneself with an awl and, at the same time, give assurances that everything is going well—that's not honest.

Such thoughts been have assailing me for a month—ever since the time I read in *Pravda* the program, or "project for a program," to organize an evening of music sponsored by the education department of the War Commissariat.

That program is propaganda, enlisting the help of music.

But how do you go about spreading propaganda through music, "whose content is pure form" (Kant)?

The result is neither scholarly nor Marxist—nothing in particular, put together by analogy, a theory concerning the existence of ideological music.

Proof of that thought would, first of all, require proving the possibility of ideological music.

And then the arranger of the musical program, with all the frivolousness characteristic of him, would make a jump and juxtapose ideological music to music written to a revolutionary plot. That is logically incorrect and not worth arguing about. It simply needs to be corrected, like a schoolboy's work. Here there has been a failure to take into account the principle of the single source. People are beginning to pound nails with a samovar.

Yes, comrades, there is music set to a revolutionary text and a samovar has weight and a certain hardness, but would this ever be sufficient to get it assigned to the category of hammers?

Alas! The very same thing is happening in painting: the strengths of the artists are occupied by posters, simply posters—not even artistically masterful posters.

I am not going to defend art in the name of art; I am going to defend propaganda in the name of propaganda.

The tsar's government knew how to put its imperial seal on everything. It applied its seal to all buttons and to all institutions.

For ten years in school I sang every morning in a herd of other children: "Save, O Lord, Thy people . . ." And yet now, and even earlier, during the year I graduated from the gymnasium, I could not recite that prayer without making a mistake. I can only sing it.

Propaganda, poured out into the air—propaganda, with which the water in the Neva is saturated—is ceasing to be felt. What is taking place is an inoculation against it, a certain immunity.

Propaganda at the opera, in cinematography, at exhibitions is useless. It devours itself.

In the name of propaganda, take propaganda out of art.

Gooseberry Jam

It seems that in one of Chekhov's plays a certain hostess plies everyone with gooseberry jam. She had cooked up several barrels-full, so she kept passing around the gooseberry jam. It had to be used up.

I think it's in *Ivanov.* I can't bring myself to read Chekhov a second time.

Evidently our theatergoers have a big supply of gooseberry jam. The things being staged are good things, with a reputation, but all this was cooked up a long time ago . . .

Delacroix has written more or less as follows: "A great man doesn't have many new ideas, but he does have one: old ideas are inadequate." Our theatergoers do not have this single idea. To tell the truth, it's absolutely wrong that a play performed on the stage be familiar to the spectator. A writer writes, for the most part anyway, to perceive something anew. But his play we perceive as restoration.

A great theater will not be a gooseberry jam theater, but one of our theaters has just created a repertory theater.

The Greeks had such a theater and the English had the theater of Shakespeare.

And Pushkin, of course, lived at his fullest when he wrote.

But now the classic writers, alas, serve only as illustrations to their commentators.

Of course, they will say, "Where in the world is our new repertory?"

If worse comes to worst, you can stage old things, but then you have to stage things not well known—not Goethe's *Faust*, but Marlowe's. Actually, though, we don't stage the things that we already have.

We do have our own great writer. Though cursed, ridiculed, unread, he has no equal. He has created a new structure and a new poetry. This is Vladimir Khlebnikov, who has a play, two even, but where can they be staged?

Gooseberry jam in the form of Shakespeare and Italian comedy, or in any other form, fills you up.

Khlebnikov is recognized by very few, but among those who recognize him are almost all poets. But for the general public, he is just a certain Futurist, to whom, like a clerk to a dog's tail, the well-known, talented Kornei Chukovsky—the Locke of Russian criticism—has fastened his critical tin can.

It is essential to stage Khlebnikov's *Death's Mistake*, which belongs to his more simply constructed things. Khlebnikov is not to blame for the fact that he's not a seventeenth-century writer or even a writer of the early nineteenth century.

There is another play that we have seen on the stage. We know its author. That is Mayakovsky's *Mystery-Bouffe*. Mayakovsky has engendered a flock of imitators, who now accuse one another in their little journals of having plagiarized him.

Mayakovsky has shoved his contemporaries aside. This is not Khlebnikov. When Mayakovsky steps on your foot and starts shouting, it's hard not to hear him.

All the same, his play, which has been staged just a few times, keeps to itself and awaits the twenty-fifth century.

I don't consider *Mystery-Bouffe* to be among Mayakovsky's best works. The ending of the play is, in my opinion, weak. It didn't come out right.

But given the flow of the dialogue, which is almost entirely structured on a pun, and given its craftsmanship, this piece deserves to be staged every day in spite of its topicality. Moreover, Mayakovsky's play is 10,000 times more rooted in folk art than all of Remizov's *Tsar Maximilian*s.

Remizov, while attempting to create a work of folk art, latched onto the outer trappings of the plot, which, as is well known, is degenerate and certainly not characteristic of folklore. Vladimir Mayakovsky took—intuitively, of course—the very device of folk drama. Folk drama is entirely founded on the word, as on the material, on word-play, on playing with words.

In the brilliant pages of *Mystery* (the opening tones are especially good), the folk device is canonized.

In order to stage Khlebnikov, it is essential to be understanding, to be skillful and to be daring, but I don't understand what troves of understanding and skill all these cohorts of workers and peasants with no repertory possess when they ignore Mayakovsky's plays, which are realized with such talent.

Is it really possible that for a long time to come our ration will consist of—gooseberry jam?

A Flag Is Snapping

Almost every district has its own little theater. Almost every organization has a theater. We even have a school that teaches students about the theater, with a special division attached to the Baltic fleet, which trains students to be prompters.

The result is something reminiscent of Evreinov's theatricalization of life.

I wouldn't be surprised if the Murmansk railroad or the Nail Combine began training actors not for itself but for export.

Music is playing; a flag is snapping.

As for nine-tenths of these theaters, no one has written a word about them. It's—"theater for the sake of theater."

I attended some of those theaters. The spirit of the telegrapher Nadkin drifted over them. The worst kind of theater used to be the theater organized by various amateurs to be performed at dachas. That kind of theater is surviving under the aegis of the Administration of Cultural Education. The spectator is being degraded, turned into a receiver of cultural tastes on the level of a former regimental clerk.

How could I, of all people, not have known that the year dominated by the dictatorship of the avant-grade and the young in art had ended? Another line had entered the scene—business-like and economically oriented. Go to the studio and you will see that the young artists have remained young and have remained leftists except for those who have stopped being young.

"Business-like art," "art that is accessible to Red Army men" is promoted by those who don't know that someone who doesn't speak in verse speaks in prose and he who rejects the new art creates art that is old and out of date.

Among them are the people who are personally well intentioned, people of "good taste"—incidentally, the worst kind for artists—but these people are devoid of life. Beside them are people a little worse and, together with the old form, burst out with: "First they died; then they got married." Music is playing, a flag is snapping and the Nail Combine is transforming workers into actors.

This hysterical obsession with acting is enveloping the entire Soviet Union like an adipose resurgence of tissues.

As to where the guilt lies, it is easy to blame the temptation of cheap art.

I am proposing to found a "League for the Protection of Red Army Men from Vaudeville, Dance and the Reading of Lectures on Cosmology."

We have announced the principle of a vocational school not for children, but for adults, instead of introducing them to the processes of scholarly work, we are using the theater in doses that would kill a horse and dishing out lectures stupefying in their superficialities—lectures at which, it seems, it is necessary to post guards at the door to keep people from leaving. And that's not just a surmise.

I remember how attentively and joyfully the Red Army soldiers listened to me at the front when it was late in the evening, since the day was busy with military work. In the darkness (there was never any light) I began to teach arithmetic to them.

People were joyful from the sensation that they were starting from scratch, that they had donned a harness and were plowing.

We need to devote all our strength to educational work, to systematic work. Such work is possible everywhere.

We need to announce a new motto: "Let's take a break from the theater" and replace these cultural boondoggles with systematic work.

This requires a lot of effort. To get the intensity needed and the speed of educational work in the troops, it's necessary to organize the classes into small groups of ten to fifteen people.

And something else is necessary: to constantly set oneself a manageable and an achievable goal. The Baltic fleet could graduate teachers instead of prompters if Narkompros won't do it. And then it will be possible and necessary to introduce the conception of art as work, as meaningful activity—and not as pretty pictures and not as games.

The old regime was unable to compartmentalize work. When some military plant was building a ship, it prepared for this work door handles and commodes.

Now we are experiencing the very same mania: "Anyone can be a corkmaker," "anyone can be an actor." The Nail Combine is preparing an artist. Meanwhile a flag is snapping.

The Appeasers

A witch doctor is not a man lacking in theory: the witch doctor has an untrue, more often than not, outmoded theory.

The performance that I attended at the Heroic Revolutionary Theater had form, all right, but it was old, very poor form.

In art there is no improvisation or, to be more precise, improvisation is possible only as a change of form, as its appearance, finally, in a *new* context.

It's impossible to make a cannon by inspiration; it's just as impossible to perform a play by instinct, by visceral impulses. A play can only be made. Revolutionary theater wanted to be a theater of *elan,* of inspiration, but it wasn't able to get by without technique. It declined to seek it out. That opened the door to the old, secondhand, discarded technique of opera and bad films. The performance went along those ruts.

It was sad to see the talented actress Chekan in such an awful play (*The Legend of a Communard*), in such trite groups and poses.

The performance in its entirety seemed to be composed of postcards and illustrations from *Native Land* (there was such a journal).

Here there was no lack of skill, there was no revolutionary overcoming of form. No, in fact, what I saw before me was the provincial tradition of form in all its inviolability.

People are not telling the truth when they justify what they do by saying that common people need a certain special, watered-down art. Folk riddles and proverbs are orchestrated in an unusually subtle way.

The stylistic devices of the Russian folk tale are no simpler than the prose devices of Andrei Bely and the audiences understand very well the devices of the folk tale, distinguishing, for example, alliteration. The factory song absorbed within itself the devices of the old Russian epic song. Since this is, of course, unknown to many who study proletarian creative work, I suggest that they scrutinize at least the song "Marusya Has Poisoned Herself." Indeed, even the chastushka is a thing that is "made, constructed."

The Legend of a Communard is a revolutionary *Vampuka*. And the individual forging the heart of the Communard is rather like Wagner, as understood from the libretto.

I don't believe that the author of *The Legend of a Communard* is a proletarian, since a fresh class, having not yet developed its possibilities, would have never picked out this man. In order to express the pathos of the proletarian revolution, he would have needed an astrologer's cap and Gabriel's sword.

I feel sorry for the people taking part in this play. It and the "witch doctor" production spoil everything, make it awkward and heavy-handed.

Drama and Mass Productions

Adrian Piotrovsky, in *News of the Petrosoviet,* proposes using drama circles in order to organize cadres to take part in mass productions.

In truth, no one knows what to do with drama circles, which are multiplying like infusoria. Neither the absence of fuel, nor the absence of foodstuffs, nor the Entente— nothing can stop their development.

In vain do the terrified leaders suggest the most varied means of replacing the circles—the circles won't budge.

"And what if they shut you down?"

"We will stage it secretly."

So Russia acts and acts. Some sort of elemental process is taking place in which living tissues are turned into the-ater tissues.

Here Evreinov enters the picture and declares: "Every minute of our life is theater." Now, why does that matter to us when we have theater every minute!

Piotrovsky's desire to make use of these theater circles in this business is understandable. He wants to straighten them out, drag them away at least from vaudeville, from summer stock, from the theater of masquerade with its multiple changes of costume.

I think that this is impossible. The fact of the matter is

that theater circles want to change costumes all the time and want to perform masquerades. Such a masquerade, performed at the House of Arts, displeased a certain man with a Browning "mask" and a very high number, received obviously later than October.*

Life is difficult. There is no way to hide its difficulty from oneself. And in this difficult life aren't we like the Selenites (the first people on the moon), seated in barrels. The only thing allowed to grow there is a tentacle, useful for the collective.

A man couldn't help being happy there where everything was softer, where people were beaten only with soft pillows and drowned without fail in warm water, but the road to yesterday was, of course, closed.

And so a man runs to the theater, to actors. In that way, according to Freud, in coping with a psychosis, we hide in some sort of mania as in a monastery, that is, we create for ourselves an illusory life, an illusory reality, instead of the hard reality that is real.

You remember, in all likelihood, the description of the theater in Dostoevsky's *Notes from the House of the Dead* to cover one's shaved head with a wig, to get dressed in gray clothing, to cross over into another life—that's what drew the convicts to the theater. Dostoevsky says that they made good actors. That's owing to the fact that in the old days, penal servitude extracted the strongest individuals.

The folk mass production, the display of strength, the joy of the crowd is a confirmation of today and its apotheosis.

---

*Under the pseudonym "Browning No.——," a certain journalist published in *Krasnaya gazeta* a nasty feuilleton about the "House of Arts."

It is legitimate when no one looks at it from a window or from a special tribune; otherwise, it degenerates into a parade, into a serf ballet and into an orchestra of horn music. And by then it is neither a masquerade nor theater.

The folk mass production is a matter for the living, whereas the drama circles are psychoses, escape, a Selenite's dream of limbs.

It would be wrong to shut down these millions of circles. It would be wrong to forbid an individual to rant and rave. They are the rash indicating a sickness and, as such, they deserve the attention of a sociologist.

But it would be wrong to use them for the construction of a new social life.

It would be wrong to build on the delirium of a deserter.

That would be too cruel.

Papa—That's an Alarm Clock

I was at the Zon Theater to see Meyerhold and Bebutov's production of Verhaeren's *Dawns* in Chulkov's adaptation, or in Meyerhold and Chulkov's adaptation or, anyway, in someone's adaptation.

The footlights had been removed. The stage was stripped bare . . . The theater was like a coat with the collar ripped off. It was not cheerful and not bright.

On the stage was a counter-relief, with stretched cables moving upward with pieces of bent iron. All of this was against a background of such blackness that it was almost not visible. This appealed to me—and would have more so if it hadn't kept me from seeing several shaved heads of people without any makeup on and in costumes representing something halfway between a counter-relief and a commissar's costume (jodhpurs).

Behind the scenes someone was beating on an iron sheet and shouting in a theatrical way. In theater jargon that signifies an uprising.

There were fifteen people in the orchestra pit: a man in civilian clothes, men, women. Judging by the way they spoke, which was like the way the actor Mgebrov spoke, these people had come from the Proletkult. Mgebrov himself was standing on a prism, but he was a prophet and therefore he spoke very loudly.

The people wearing sport coats in the orchestra were supposed to mingle with the public. In order to facilitate that development, the footlights had been removed.

As for the text itself, Verhaeren has written a bad play. Since revolutionary theater is created in great haste, the play had been accepted in great haste, since people in great haste had assumed it to be a revolutionary play.

As for the content of the play, it's a story about how the leader, Rene, formed a coalition with the bourgeoisie.

The text of the play has been changed. The people on stage talk about the Union of Action, the Power of the Soviets. The action has been modernized, though I don't know why the imperialistic forces are going into battle with shields and lances.

In the middle of the second act, it seems, a messenger arrives and reads a telegram concerning the losses of the Red Army at Perekop.

Obviously, this is artistically based on the insinuation of the tragedy of life into the tragedy of art. But since the whole plot is brought up to date, the telegram does not stand out of its text and the artistic effect on which it is based fails.

Music is playing, the members of the Proletkult in the orchestra are shouting, on stage people are singing a funeral march. The public gets to its feet . . . and stands there. The mass meeting is a debacle.

The idea of the directors was that this show would involve three groups of players—the actors (stage), the members of the Proletkult (the orchestra) and the public (parterre), but the public is out on strike.

In a real mass meeting, the public behaves more vigorously than at one conducted in a play.

The biggest mistake of the evening was that the play, admittedly bad, was utterly destroyed by the mass meeting element. It was a failure. Equally bad was the conflict between this element and the rest of the play.

For this conflict to have had a successful outcome, it would have been necessary to keep the play intact and to rupture its immobile body with excerpts from contemporary writers.

Teffi has a story about an unsuccessful inventor, constantly trying to figure out what he would like to invent.

Early one morning, having overslept, he sets out to get some tea: "It would be nice to invent some little machine that would tell you when to wake up and it would wake you up . . ."

However, the daughter interrupts him: "But, Papa, that's an alarm clock!"

Collective Creativity

The question of collective creativity has emerged into the bright field of consciousness manifested by contemporary society.

Collective creativity, of course, is understood by many very naïvely. For example, this week one of our newspapers published a note announcing the forthcoming production of a play written collectively by four authors; moreover, each author has written his own act.

Of course, such creativity is completely possible. We know the novels of Erckmann and Chatrian, the brothers Goncourt. Alexandre Dumas *père* maintained in his home a regular factory for the preparation of novels and Sardou ordered helpers to prepare separate scenes of his plays, while he himself only connected and polished them.

But all these instances are not so much collective creativity as they are group collectivity.

Real collectivity in creative work is deeper but also broader.

In granting patents for inventions, a clerk writes down not only the day but the hour, even the minute in which the application is awarded. Experience has shown that it's entirely possible that another inventor, with the very same invention, will appear. That's what happened with the invention of the telephone.

On the whole, gaining priority over an invention or a discovery is very hard. The epoch has prepared the premises of a structure and several people, having no connection with one another, feel themselves to be creators. In this instance, a human being and the human brain are none other than a geometric point where lines of collective creativity intersect.

I will explain my idea with a comparison. If we take a completely motionless glass of water and throw some fine old powder into it, we will see that, as soon as the water grows still, the minute particles of the powder suspended in the water will move, as a swarm of gnats moves in the sun, but much more quietly. This is called Brownian Motion, from the name of the scientist who discovered it and who explained to us that the minute particles suspended in liquid, by virtue of the insignificance of their mass, perceive the movement of the molecules and begin to vibrate under the action of their jolts.

The creator—be it the inventor of the internal combustion engine or a poet—plays the role of such particles, which make motions—invisible by themselves—visible.

Many readers may know how actors perform, or used to perform, the Italian comedies of improvisation, the so-called "Commedia dell'arte." You take a scenario. At the base of the scenario is deposited some sort of plot. The plots, as you know, are not the product of an individual creator. They move from one temporary stratum occupied by creators of art to another, changing under the influence of the desire constantly to make material capable of being experienced palpably. Onto that base actors interpolate their jokes, enlivening and beautifying traditional lines. But everyone listening to, and telling, jokes knows that these jokes also represent a storehouse of spare parts, and in that way the artist-improvisor interpolates onto a traditional—in the broad sense of that word—frame the traditional realization. An epic singer also creates this way.

In the same way the creation of the story of folk tales was described by Rybnikov. He spoke about the storehouse common to all storytellers.

It seems to us that our so-called individual creation is accomplished not that way, but that it is a result of impossibility or, more accurately, the difficulty of seeing the present day in general.

We feel that the lyric poetry of the Middle Ages operates out of the scholarly tradition, that the chivalric novel, for example, is a rearrangement of all those worn-out patterns, but from these same schemata we feel, finally, that the post-revolutionary stories in Russian literature are also traditional, as are stories based on the "gender problem," but we don't feel that even now we are operating with the traditional collective creativity. By the word collective here I understand not the entire mass of the population but a society of bards and writers not dependent on whether we are speaking about so-called folk creativity or about so-called artistic creativity.

Pushkin and Gogol are the same sort of phenomenon in their school, just as is an ordinary writer. We isolate them from the masses, because we are unable to perceive them as part of a continuous process. We need a new word.

Creativity—even the revolutionary-artistic type—is traditional creativity. Violating the canon is possible only when a canon exists, and blasphemy presupposes a religion that hasn't yet perished.

There exists a "church" of art in the sense of a gathering of those who feel it. This church has its canons, created by the accumulation of heresies.

Worrying about the creation of collective art is just as futile as worrying about the fact that the Volga flows into the Caspian Sea.

In My Own Defense

I'm not trying to tease anyone when I write about Tolstoy. History is perfect. Any phenomenon is more understandable when we can understand the process of its origin. All around us are many matters demanding rapid decisions, but in order to decide, it's necessary to know what I have to say about worker-peasant art to an individual who knows nothing, not only about the laws of art, but about the material itself and the works of art themselves.

I'm not a literary con-man and I'm not a magician. All I can give to the leaders of the masses are those formulas which will help make sense of newly appearing phenomena—after all, the new develops according to old laws. It's painful for me to read the rebukes of *Pravda* and it's offensive to be referred to as "Mister." I'm not a "Mister." I've been Comrade Shklovsky for five years now. My comrades who, along with me, write for a newspaper deserve above all else respect and not rebukes. We are not hacks. We work from primary sources and we take our work very seriously. The fact that we write articles on Schiller and Sterne, solving problems anew, is a miracle.

Comrade from *Pravda*, this is not an apology. This is an assertion of my right to be proud.

We are too preoccupied by knowledge; we get too carried away by the popularization of science; we think too little about productivity in science; we haven't made a place for it.

My comrades and I work by the light of oil lamps when the temperature is 32 degrees Fahrenheit. We will work by torchlight and we will work when the temperature is below zero, but only as we can. We know where we're going.

Regarding Psychological Footlights[*]

Comrade Kerzhentsev has raised the question of a "theater without spectators," a theater of action—an improvisational theater.

I am absolutely in agreement with Derzhavin's article and with his idea that such theaters always existed, but that they were simply not regarded as theater. The word theater signified something completely different. What matters in the theater is theatricality.

Hoffmann in "The Princess Bramboulle" made use of the following device. One of the characters in the story says, "We are all characters in 'Cappricchio,' which is now being written." Here there is an interesting orientation to the "artificiality of the action," with emphasis on its conventionality.

This device can be found in Cervantes's *Don Quixote*, where an insane man reads a story about himself. That sort of thing is very characteristic of Sterne and for almost everyone in the Romantic School, which, at its base, by the way, is a school which emphasizes and revives the conventionality of form.

The same device, but bent to the other side of realized conventionality, we see in Gogol's *Dead Souls* when he

_____
[*]Written in response to Bystryansky's articles in *Pravda*.

advises the reader not to repeat loudly Chichikov's name in case Chichikov would hear it and take offense.

There was an instance in a small German town when, as a tragedy was being performed, the spectators jumped up on stage and, by force, stopped the "bloodbath."

One of my female acquaintances, during a performance of a melodrama—*Two Orphans,* I believe—started shouting at the actors and looking for an exit: "Out the window! Out the window!"

In these instances the illusion was overcome, but the theater has no need of that. What the theater needs is a flickering illusion, that is, one that comes and goes.

Psychological footlights are one of the stylistic devices of the theater, one of the elements of its form.

There are works of art built entirely on playing with the footlights—Arthur Schnitzler's *The Green Parrot* for example, or *Pagliacci.* Here the idea is that the action is perceived sometimes as real, sometimes as illusory.

But emphasis on the footlights is encountered not only in these plays.

In Shakespeare's *King Lear* the king is offended by his daughter, turns to the audience and addresses a lady sitting in the parterre: "Why, nature needs not what thou gorgeous wear'st which scarcely keeps thee warm."

In Ostrovsky's *A Family Affair* a man insulted by a clerk hurls himself toward the footlights and shows the audience his worn shoes, complaining to the onlookers about Podkhalyuzin. A similar device is canonical in vaudeville.

The Romantics made wide use of this device in their theatrical productions. That explains all these theater directors in the plays of Tieck and Hoffmann (Zhirmunsky).

All these bared devices that involve playing with the footlights demonstrate their importance in the structure of drama.

To destroy the psychological footlights would be no different from destroying, well, for example, alliteration in poetry.

Speaking in a Loud Voice

When I have occasion to write theatrical reviews, I feel like the state seal which Mark Twain's Tom, having made himself King of England, used to crack nuts.

With regard to the theater, and art in general, it's better not to write reviews—it's better to create studies, to work in groups, in scientific societies, and, finally, having found the basis of scientific poetics, allow oneself to speak—and then, to speak loudly.

But it's also necessary to crack nuts.

It's necessary to write if only to keep someone else from taking your place and from tormenting you with his wit.

With such stipulations I'm writing about the performance of the mystery play that took place in the portals of the stock exchange.

I saw only the dress rehearsal, so I will have to speak in fragments.

I liked a lot of things about this production—above all, that a parade was introduced into the structure of the "Mystery" as an organic component. The result is a very interesting duality. "Artistically," that is, according to the laws of art, the structured movement of the masses, the enslaved and rebellious people are equated with the "prosaic," that is, according to the laws of usefulness by the structured movements of the troops.

This is the use of non-aesthetic material in a work of art.

This made more of an impact on me than the numerical immensity of the mass in the mystery.

That was devised by someone with talent.

One can create works of art in that way, but it would have been much more daring to use juxtaposition, to find the aesthetic relation not between the "aesthetic" and the non-aesthetic subject, but between two non-aesthetic subjects, directly between objects of the real world.

I think that one could create a work of art by contrasting the Vyborg side of town with the Petersburg side.

An attack on the "kingdom of freedom" is a better and stronger part of the performance. Much weaker in terms of suspense is a "circus chorus of kings."

In order to contrast a human body with a human crowd, it's necessary to somehow *heroize* it or else relate to it more attentively than is our wont.

The scale of the production is fine—fine, as I was told, if you introduce searchlights from the Fortress of Peter and Paul. Fine when such a big piece of the city and its water take part in the spectacle. Maybe the scale of the production could be expanded in its composition to include the whole city, along with St. Isaac's Cathedral and the balloon over Uritsky Square.

In such a spectacle the construction cranes over the Neva should play leading roles as precursors of my brothers, the Martians of H. G. Wells. And a searchlight would simultaneously direct all the orchestras in the city, turning all the cannons into drums.

I envy the producers of "mysteries."

It's a pleasure to speak in a loud voice if one has a loud voice.

THE VISUAL ARTS

Regarding "The Great Metalworker"

It rose and hung in the air for a while, the question about the casting in bronze of "The Great Metalworker," the work of the sculptor Blokh. I have no idea who came up with the grandiloquent name of this statue. Perhaps this question should be left unanswered, since the statue is very bad—bad not only from the point of view of a Futurist but bad from all points of view and bad because now it's impossible to make a good statue "of the old school."

There are various means of creating art objects. Various artistic forms do not exist simultaneously. When Rodin wanted to copy antique statues, it seemed that he kept making them too gaunt, but he himself noticed that only by means of measurement. Various epochs are capable of feeling various things and every epoch has things closed to its perception. *Let us remember that Titus Livy saw mountains only as ugly.* The perception of the human body went from the sphere of visibility to the sphere of recognition. At least the body is not changed, not transformed, not disfigured, not decomposed. It does not exist as a subject of artistic perception. It is not for nothing that in our language there are almost no words having to do with the parts of the body. And our children, when they draw, always draw button-like forms, and almost never draw knees and elbows. One can by inertia model men and even make them huge and even call them great, but a simple measurement of the work of an honest artisan, Ilya Ginzburg or Blokh, if you like, will show that they have been modeled by people who did not see them, but only know by heart that a man has a head, arms and even legs.

Those who do not want to seek, but prefer to clip coupons of the old traditions, think that they are representatives of the old school.

They're mistaken. It's impossible to create in forms already established since creativity is change.

Tolstoy was a classic writer and he laughed at those who failed to understand why the old forms, which had been good for Pushkin or Gogol, were bad for imitators, who used them as something ready-made.

The fact is that the so-called old art doesn't exist, doesn't have an objective existence, and therefore it's impossible to make a work of art according to its rules.

The history of art is not a library where one can take from the shelf any book one wants: a book from yesterday's publications or a book from Gutenberg's time.

Art of the past lives or dies. It blazes up or falls down into a pitiful existence of collections, where everything is of equal value: both paintings and cigarettes with strange cigarette holders: "the kind that you can't get anymore."

Actually, this is expressed in the fact that all the great architects were destroyers. They destroyed a church with a hipped roof in order to build in its place a new stone church. Tomon de Thomon destroyed Giacomo Quarenghi's Stock Exchange in order to put his own in Quarenghi's place. Quarenghi destroyed many, Bartolomeo Rastrelli destroyed many. The summer palace erected by Rastrelli himself was destroyed in order to put in its place his magnificent Engineers' Castle. Bazhenov wanted to tear down the Kremlin and substitute in its place his own structure. Only as shadows, only as a perception of an antiquary, can there co-exist structures of various epochs. A living artist destroys because he sees only his own work.

The monks did the right thing when they erased Virgil's poems from the parchment in order to write their chronicles and paint their miniatures.

This happens not because the forms of life are changing or because the forms of production relations are changing.

Change in art is not the result of changes in daily life. Change in art results from old forms becoming petrified, the endless passage of things from tactile perception to habitualized recognition.

All these artists of the "Obshchina," all these "Wanderers"—that's not old art. That's nothing but dead blotches, rotting tree stumps. All that is as dead as the recurrent epithet.

Every artistic form undergoes a journey from birth to death, from visibility and sensual perception, when a thing projects admiration and emerges into visibility in every twist and turn toward recognition, when the thing, the form becomes a dull imitator of memory and tradition, becoming invisible to the client himself.

Blokh and the Blokhovites make things which are not palpable, which are devoid of palpability and which do not exist artistically, just as certain things have ceased to be perceived as artistic objects, "antimacassars" and "vases" on buffets. Equally dead now and so garbled, used with such a complete disregard of structure is the arch, which is being stuck haphazardly onto monuments to the revolution.

In Russia there is bronze and there are many people who do not understand art, but who are voting to have the "Bronze Metalist" converted from a gypsum scarecrow into a bronze scarecrow, but this will not turn its "memorized" forms into artistic forms.

Of course, it could be cast, it could even be gilded . . .

It's a great pity to see the energy being wasted to remove Berenstein's monument and to erect Blokh's monument. Anyone can see that this is a deliberate, full-fledged, artistically made situation of going from the frying pan into the fire. It may be that the proletariat is as yet unable to perceive the forms of avant-garde art. The bourgeoisie failed to understand the artists of their time, but that doesn't give anyone the right to force on the proletariat copper buttons instead of gold, and Blokh instead of sculpture.

Space in Painting and the Suprematists

Historical materialism is fine for sociology, but it's impossible to use it as a substitute for a knowledge of mathematics and astronomy. It's impossible to rely wholly on historical materialism in designing a bridge or in defining the laws by which the comets move.

It's equally impossible to proceed from historical materialism to explain and reject, or accept, a work of art or a whole school in art. Therefore I'm trying to explain the phenomena of art: "An oak tree grows out of an acorn."

The goal of the visual arts is, and will be, the creation of artistic things, i.e., artistic forms. If we had wanted in the visual arts to "imitate nature," it would have been an attempt with unworthy means toward an unworthy end. For example, Helmholtz proved that the relation of the force of light between a piece of the sky and the shadow of a forest can be expressed as the relation 20,000 to one. In a painting, however, the difference between the brightest and darkest spots cannot be more than 60 to one. In that way the painting with its colors cannot convey the relation of light, but that is not the task of a painting. A painting is something constructed according to its own laws, and not the result of imitation.

Now about form. People usually think that, thanks to perspective, we can on the painting's surface convey the form of an object. That opinion is wrong.

In the first place, perspective, even the most academic, is not a structure according to the law of descriptive geometry. In a big painting, for example, the edges are drawn in such a way as if the observer were standing right in front of them, and not in front of the center of the painting. In that way, the objects depicted on such a painting are given from two or more points of view.

From that fact flows the "law" of academic painting: not to shorten the horizontal feature of the lines. Therefore in depicting the interior of a building, painters use one kind of reduction, whereas a group of people, located in that building, are fleshed out according to a different reduction, according to other laws. One can learn about this even in the encyclopedic dictionary, which I advise as a minimal program for people who are now writing half-baked articles about art.

In the second place, if the painting is hung on a wall, but not at the level at which it was painted, and if these matters were not carefully calculated by the artist (the usual case with an easel painting), then the line of the horizon on the painting will seem false. That is the situation in which almost all the paintings in our museums find themselves. However, even in the process of completion, the paintings sometimes (especially in the case of Veronese) are painted with two or more lines of the horizon.

But even if perspective had followed the laws of descriptive geometry, even then it would not have been able to convey forms objectively.

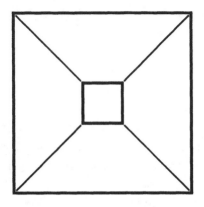

Now let's imagine a small square inside a big one. Let's connect their corners. Now we will look, fixing our attention on the small square. We will see that before us is depicted a truncated pyramid with a square foundation, turned with its apex toward us.

Then let's fix our attention on the big square. We will see the same pyramid, but now turned toward us with its foundation, as it were, cut into it on the inside.

If we now throw a fleeting glance at the drawing, without emphasizing by our attention a single one of the contours, we will not experience palpability of form. This experiment was analyzed by Wundt and then worked out in detail as applied by Christiansen to painting in his *Philosophy of Art*.

I'm not in complete agreement with several of Christiansen's conclusions, but I don't want to analyze them in this article. For now I will say only that our drawing is an outline with perspective. The big square can be considered a foreground; the small one a background. But it can also be done the other way around. One can, as we saw, turn the drawing inside out and present the rear plane as the forward one.

Finally, one can flatten the drawing, perceive it as flat.

In that way, and from this side, perspective is conventional. It's based on the tradition of impediment.

European painting canonized the second instance, that is, the perspective of converging parallels. Japanese and Byzantine painting canonized the first instance, which gave rise to so-called reverse perspective. Frescoes and mosaics are constructed according to a third means, in which, strictly speaking, depth is absent. Accordingly, a drawing is hung flat on the wall. Frescoes are painted right on the wall, but a painting is torn away from the wall, hanging at an angle and suggesting to the eye the perception of space by means of a beveled frame.

As we see, even space in the visual arts is a convention, a pictorial convention. And this is just as true for academics as it is for Futurists.

Accordingly, it is totally wrong to replace a mosaic with a "copy" made, for example, from oil paints, since the principles involved in the construction of space in these two "painting systems" are completely different.

The tsarist regime was on the verge of making just such a mistake in St. Isaac's Cathedral by replacing paintings in the Italian manner (not a fresco) with copies made of mosaics. Now these projects have been halted.

But neither direct nor reverse perspective explains the structure of a painting.

Paintings are formed by their "objectness." Let me explain my assertion. If we take a man who has been blind from birth and remove the cataracts from his eyes and restore his sight, he will not see the world as a series of objects arranged one after another in space. The world presents itself to him in the form of colored shutters and colored curtains, lying directly near his eyes (Ribot). Only muscular experience teaches us to construct space around ourselves in the outer world.

Therefore, when we see an object, palpability of form occurs only when we recognize the object, when we recognize it for what it is.

Hildebrandt in his book *Problems of Form* points out that in order to create the impression of depth and height in a painting, it's not enough to depict a receding field. It's essential, for example, to sketch in that field a tree, which will then be shown to cast a shadow. The shadow will suggest to us the depth of the painting.

In exactly the same way, if we see on a Grecian vase or on a modern cup, the black silhouette of some body or other, sometimes even given in foreshortening, it is only after we connect it with an idea of what it may be—the contour of a goat, for example—only then do we perceive volume.

In addition, if the contour allows not one, but several interpretations, then the multiple objects of these interpretations will give us several contradictory interpretations.

In this way the material of the painting is usually not paints but a bright depiction of objects.

In the history of art (Grosse) the gravitation from the animal and vegetable ornament to the geometric is an established fact.

That fact may be connected with the phenomenon which Meiman pointed out: in children's drawings, form does not appear until they can construct for themselves a certain conception (not scientific) of geometric form.

In any case, the geometric-Cubist style takes hold of art periodically. One of these takeovers took place in Greece, apparently after the epoch of black-figure depiction. A cup with a geometric type of drawing may be found, by the way, in the Hermitage.

As the depiction becomes more geometric, objects quickly disassociate themselves from each other, turning into an abstract design.

Having torn ourselves away from this "objectness," with objects, we lose one of the reasons for the creation of forms and we arrive at flat depictions. In this way, the "objectness" in the work of the Suprematists and their repudiation of space are closely connected with one another.

Giotto wrote that for him a painting was above all an alternation of colorful surfaces. But only the Suprematists, through long work on the object, as on the material, realized what the elements of the painting are. Only the Suprematists freed themselves from the slavery of things. And, having bared the device, they presented the painting to the observer only as a colored flat surface.

I do not think that paintings will always remain abstract, artists have not been striving all this time toward the fourth dimension in order to remain in two dimensions. But for me the ancestors of the Suprematists are clear, as are the inevitability and necessity of this movement. If artists return to the depiction of objects or even to a preoccupation with plot—which in our understanding of the word, that is, in the sense of creating a stepped structure, as the Futurists do—(those occasions when they deconstruct the object into planes) it is then and only then that the Suprematists' work will be seen not to have been undertaken in vain.

Regarding Texture and Counter-Reliefs

It often behooves one to read complaints about the difficulty of expressing one's thought in art.

Poets have filled their poems with these complaints. Gornfeld, feeling sorry for the poor poets, has written an article called "Torments of the Word."

To look at the form of art, that is, at art itself, as at an interpreter translating the thoughts of the artist from the language of his soul into a language comprehensible to the spectator is a commonplace. For those who support such a view, "the word" in literature is "a color" in the painting—a regrettable necessity. From these "means" available to artists have been demanded, above all else, transparency and intelligibility. Artists have paid lip service to these demands, but in their studios they have gone their own way.

What makes art enchanting?

The outside world does not exist. Equally nonexistent, and equally imperceptible, are things replaced by words, and non-existent are words which are hardly used, hardly pronounced.

The outside world is outside of art. Art is perceived as a series of hints, a series of algebraic signs, as a collection of things having volume, but no substance—texture.

Texture is the main feature of that special world of especially constructed things, the aggregate of which we usually call art.

The word in art and the word in life are profoundly different. In life it plays the role of a bead on an abacus, in art it's a texture. We have it in sound. It reverberates and we listen to it in its full potential.

In life we fly over the world as Jules Verne's heroes flew from the earth to the moon in a closed sphere but in our sphere there are no windows. The entire work of the artist-poet and the artist-painter consists first and foremost in creating a continuous palpable thing, a textured thing.

A poet having as the material of his creation formal structures—not only the word-sound but also the word-concept—also creates from it new things. Good and evil in art are textures. It is wrong to think that art, as it changes, gets better. The very concept of improvement as a rising upward is anthropomorphic.

The forms of art replace one another.

There are minutes when, if art has not declined, it has absorbed a set of elements alien to it. Such, for example, is the work of our Wanderers.

In that case, art lives despite those elements, which take part in its life as a bullet in the chest takes part in the life of the body.

It's wrong to say that Repin is a lousy artist, but it is necessary to remember that he is an artist to the extent that he has decided questions about the creation of a special breed of things—a canvas covered with paint.

On the other hand, artists, often thinking that they are resolving purely artistic problems are, in fact, not resolving them but merely showing off. The result is the corollary of algebra in painting, that is, an "unmade painting"—a thing essentially prosaic. To such symbolism in painting it is necessary to relegate the school of the Suprematists.

Their paintings are rather "cooked up" than made. They aren't organized by taking account of the continuous nature of perception.

True, here the "question posed" is not about the harmfulness of religion or serfdom, but about the relation of a red rectangle to a white background but, in fact, this is a painting oriented to ideas, too.

Of all the Russian artists, there are two who, more than anyone else, have addressed the question of how to create fabricated, continuous things—Tatlin and Altman.

Altman has done this in a series of paintings in which he has bared the orientation to the texture, where the whole concept of paintings is juxtaposed to flat planes of various roughness. Tatlin is moving away from painting.

In the academy (in the free studios of Vasily Island) I attended an exhibition of things from Tatlin's studio. Unfortunately, I didn't see his own work—the model of the Monument to the Third International.

The model will be shown in November, at which time we will be able to speak of it concretely.

For the time being, though, we can say that Tatlin has left paintings and pictures, which he made so well, in order to move into contrasting one object, taken just as it is, to another.

I did see the work of one of Tatlin's students. It's a big square of parquet, developed in such a way that its pieces vary in texture and present, in a manner of speaking, several surfaces moving away from one another. One piece of the square is occupied by a piece of copper of irregular form, to which are juxtaposed strips of tracing paper, fastened in front of the basic plane of the work.

The ultimate task for Tatlin and his students is, obviously, the creation of a new world of palpability, the transference or dissemination of the methods by which to construct artistic things, "things of daily life." The ultimate goal of such a movement is to construct a tangible new world.

A counter-relief, a sketch, pieces of some sort of special paradise where there are no names and no voids, where life is like our life today—a "flight in a sphere," from one point to another like traveling on an invisible road, from station to station.

The new world should be a continuous world.

I don't know whether Tatlin is right or wrong, I don't know whether the bent tin-plate leaves of his students' compositions will be able to blossom in the forged counter-reliefs of a new world.

I don't believe in miracles. That's why I'm not an artist.

The Monument to the Third International
(Tatlin's Most Recent Work)

The days run together like train cars overflowing with strange and variegated vehicles, cannons, crowds yelling about something or other. The days thunder like a pile driver, blow after blow, and the blows have already blended and ceased to be heard, just as people living by the sea don't hear the sound of the water. The blows thunder somewhere in the chest below consciousness.

We are living in the quiet of thunder.

In this paved air has been born the iron spiral of a project: a monument the size of two Cathedrals of St. Isaac's.

This spiral, which is leaning on its side, is prevented from collapsing by its powerful, diagonally standing form.

Such a basic structure of the project for a monument to the Third International is the work of the artist Tatlin.

The twists and turns of the spiral are united by a network of leaning stanchions. In their transparent hollow turn three geometric bodies. Below moves a cylinder with a speed of one turn a year; the pyramid above it turns once a month and the ball at the apex completes a full turn every day. The waves of the radio station standing at the very apex continue the monument into the air.

Here for the first time iron is standing on its hind legs and seeking its artistic formula.

In the age of construction cranes, as fine as the wisest Martian, iron has the right to go on a rampage and to remind people that our "age," for some reason or other, has been calling itself the "iron" age since the time of Ovid, though there was, as yet, no iron art. One could argue at length about the monument. The bodies turning in its body are small and relatively light in comparison to its enormous "general" body. Their turning itself hardly changes its appearance. It has more the character of a project than a finished product. The monument is imbued with utilitarianism. This spiral may not aspire to be an apartment building, but all the same it is somehow being put to good use.

According to the plan, in the lower cylinder we have the rotating Sovnarkom (Sovet Narodnykh Komissarov) in the shape of a globe, and in the upper cylinder we have "Rosta"(Rossiiskoe Telegrafnoe Agentstvo).

The word in poetry is not just a word. It draws in its wake dozens and thousands of associations. It is permeated with them just as the Petersburg air during a blizzard is permeated with snow.

A painter or a counter-relief artist is not free to choose in this blizzard of associations the movement across the canvas of a painting or between the stanchions of an iron spiral. These works of art have their own semantics.

The Soviet of People's Commissars has been taken by Tatlin into the monument, or so it seems to me, as new artistic material, which will be used along with "ROSTA" for the creation of artistic form.

The monument is made of iron, glass and revolution.

Ivan Puni

Ivan Puni is essentially a shy man. His hair is black, he speaks quietly. On his father's side of the family, he's Italian. Only at the movies did he see on the screen quiet, shy people.

A house painter with a long ladder on his shoulder, is walking down the street. He's modest and quiet. But the ladder catches on people's hats, breaks glass, stops streetcars, destroys buildings.

As for Puni, he goes on painting his pictures.

If you were to collect all the reviews about him in Russia and squeeze out of them their rage, it would be possible to collect several buckets of extremely caustic liquid and, by inoculation of this liquid, infect all the dogs in Berlin with hydrophobia.

In Berlin, there are 500,000 dogs.

Puni offends people because he never teases. He paints a picture, looks at it and thinks, "What have I got to do to it? That's how it has to be."

His paintings cannot be altered and are needed.

He sees the spectator, but is organically incapable of taking him into account. He accepts the abuse of critics as one would accept a change in the weather.

While Puni lives, he makes conversation. So Columbus, sailing on his ship to undiscovered America, sat on the deck and played checkers.

Meanwhile Puni is a painter's painter. Painters don't understand him yet, but they're already nervous.

After Puni's death—and I don't want his death; we're the same age and I'm also lonely—after Puni's death, a museum will be built over his grave. In the museum will hang his pants and hat. People will say: "He was a genius and yet how modest he was. With that gray hat pulled down to his eyebrows, he was hiding the rays that emanated from his forehead."

Someone will write about his pants, too.

And really, Puni knew how to dress.

On the wall will hang the gas bill for the Puni studio. The bill will have been paid with special care. Our time will be called the "Punic era." May all those who come to cover our graves with their written praise be covered with leprosy.

In our name they will oppress future generations, the way food is compressed in a can.

The recognition of an artist is a means of neutralizing him.

And maybe there won't be a museum?

We'll do our best.

Meanwhile Puni, with his polite smile, attentively paints his pictures. He carries under his gray sport coat a furious red fox, which quietly gnaws on him. That's very painful, even though it's just a story taken from an elementary school reader.

THE LAW OF INEQUALITY

Parallels in Tolstoy

In order to make an object a fact of art, it is necessary to extricate it from the facts of life. To achieve that,
it is necessary, above all else, to shake things up, as Ivan
the Terrible "sorted out" folks. It is essential to tear the
thing from the set of customary associations in which it is
lodged. You must turn the thing like a log on the fire. In
Chekhov's *Notebook* (I don't have it at hand) there is such
an example. Someone walked down a side street each day
for either fifteen or thirty years. Every day he read a sign
he thought said, "Big Selection of Sigs" [a kind of salmon]
and every day he thought: who needs a big selection of sigs?
Finally, the sign was taken down and put on the wall side-
ways. Then he read: "Big Selection of Cigars."

A poet takes all the signs down from their places. An
artist always foments the revolt of things. In the hands
of poets, things revolt, throwing off their old names and
taking with the new name a new face. The poet uses
images, tropes, similes; he calls, let us suppose, a fire a red
blossom or he attaches to an old word a new epithet or, as
Baudelaire says, "The carrion raised its legs like a woman
for shameful caresses." In this way the poet makes a seman-
tic shift. He wrests the concept from the conceptual set in
which it stood and transfers it, with the help of a word (a

trope), to another conceptual set. Thus we feel newness, the location of the object in a new set. The new word fits the object like a new dress. The sign has been taken down. This is one of the ways of turning an object into something which may become material for a work of art. Another way is the creation of stepped form. The thing splits into its reflections and oppositions.

This way is almost universal. Stepped form serves as the basis for very many stylistic devices, such as, for example, parallelism:

> O, little apple, where are you rushing?
> Oh, Mama, I want to get married!

The poet is, in all likelihood, continuing the tradition of the following type of song:

> The little apple rushed from the other side of a bridge
> Katichka excused herself from the banquet table.

The tramp from Rostov. Here we have a pair of concepts completely at odds but shifting one another out of the set of ordinary associations.

Sometimes the thing splits into two or disintegrates. Aleksandr Blok dismembers the word *zheleznodorozhnaya* (railroad) into the words *zhelezo* and *dorozhnaya* (iron, road). Lev Tolstoy, in his works, which are as formal as music, made structures of the type called *estrangement* (calling things not by their usual name) and giving examples of stepped form.

With regard to estrangement in Tolstoy, I have had occasion to write quite a bit about it. One of the various aspects of this device consists of the fact that the writer focuses and underscores in the picture some detail which changes the usual proportions. So in a battle scene Tolstoy develops the detail of a chewing wet mouth. This turning of attention to that detail creates a peculiar shift. Konstantin Leontiev, in his wonderful book about Tolstoy, failed to understand that device. But the most common device in Tolstoy is his refusal to recognize things and his description of them as if they were being seen for the first time. He calls the stage set in *War and Peace* pieces of painted cardboard. The sacrament is performed with a bun and he assures us that that Christians eat their God.

I think that the tradition of this device goes back to French literature—perhaps to Huron the Naïve in Voltaire's "L'ingenu" or to Chateaubriand's description of the French court as seen by a savage.

In any case, Tolstoy "estranged" Wagner's things by describing them from the point of view of an intelligent peasant, that is, from the point of view of a man having no customary associations, i.e., the same type as a French barbarian. Incidentally, just such a device is used to describe a city from the point of view of a villager even in the ancient novel (Veselovsky).

The second device, the device of stepped form, was developed by Lev Tolstoy in a very distinctive way.

I won't attempt to give even a summary of that device and the process which Tolstoy used to create his distinctive poetics and will limit myself now to several remarks. The young Tolstoy constructed parallels rather naïvely. Especially when he wanted to develop the themes of dying—to show it. It seemed essential to Tolstoy to set in motion three themes:

the death of the lady of the house, the death of a peasant and the death of a tree. I'm speaking about the short story called "Three Deaths." The parts of this story are connected with a particular motivation: the peasant is this mistress's coachman and the tree is chopped down to make a cross for his grave.

In the late folk lyric, parallelism was also sometimes motivated. So, for example, the common parallel: to love = to trample the grass is motivated by the fact that the lovers have trampled the grass as they converse.

In "Kholstotmer" the parallel horse = man is underscored by the phrase, "The dead body of Serpukhovskoi, after walking and eating and drinking on earth, was put away in the ground much later. His hide, meat and bones were of no use to anyone."

The connection between the terms of the parallel is motivated in this story by the fact that Serpukhovskoi had once been Kholstomer's owner. In "Two Hussars," the parallel is seen in the very title and is developed in the details: love, card games and one's relation to friends.

A motivation that connects the parts is the kinship of the characters.

If you compare the devices of Tolstoy's craftsmanship, with Maupassant's devices, you will notice that the French craftsman omits, by implication, the second part of the parallel. This second, implied term usually proves to be the traditional structure of the novella being violated by him; for example, he writes novellas, as it were, without endings, or else, let's say, the usual conventional bourgeois-French attitude toward life. So, for example, in many of Maupassant's novellas the death of a peasant is described simply but in a surprisingly "estranged" way. Moreover, as a measure of comparison, of course, we have the literary description of the death of a city dweller, but it is not activated in this novella.

From that point of view, Tolstoy is, so to speak, more primitive than Maupassant. Tolstoy needs a parallel of revelation, as in *The Fruits of Enlightenment*—a kitchen and a parlor. I think that this is explained with greater precision in the French literary tradition as compared to the Russian. The French reader feels the violation of the canon more sharply or else finds the parallel more easily than our reader with his unclear conception of the norm.

I want to observe in passing that, speaking of literary tradition, I do not conceive of it as a borrowing by one writer from another. I imagine the tradition of a writer as a dependence on some general storehouse of literary norms, just as the tradition of an inventor amounts to the sum of technical possibilities of his time.

More complex instances of parallelism in Tolstoy's novels may be seen in the oppositions between individual characters or between groups of characters. For example, in *War and Peace* the oppositions are felt sharply:

1) Napoleon—Kutuzov,

2) Pierre Bezukhov—Andrei Bolkonsky,

and at the same time Nikolai Rostov, who serves as a sort of yardstick (standard) for one or the other.

In *Anna Karenina* the group Anna—Vronsky is opposed to the group Levin—Kitty, and the connection between these groups is motivated by kinship. This is the usual motivation in Tolstoy and also perhaps in novelists in general. Tolstoy himself wrote that he had made the "old" Bolkonsky the father of a brilliant young man (Andrei) since "it's awkward to describe a character having no connection whatsoever with the novel." Another method is to have one and the same character take part in various combinations (favored by the English novelists) but rarely used by Tolstoy except in the episode Petrushka—Napoleon, where he used it for purposes of estrangement.

In any case, the two parts of the parallel in *Anna Karenina* are connected by an incredibly weak motivation: one can only assume that the connection is motivated by artistic necessity.

It is very interesting to see how Tolstoy uses "kinship" not for the motivation of the connection but for the creation of stepped form. In the Rostov family, we see two brothers and one sister. They represent an elaboration of a certain type. Sometimes, as for example, in the section that precedes the death of Petya, he compares them. Nikolai Rostov is a simplification of Natasha, a "coarse" version of her. Stiva Obolensky opens one side of the structure of Anna Karenina's soul—the connection of home through the word *nemnozhectvo* [a smidgen], which Anna says in Stiva's voice. Stiva is a "step" toward his sister.

Here the connection between the characters is not explained by kinship. Tolstoy was not too shy to link on the pages of the novel separately conceived heroes. In this case kinship was needed for the construction of the steps.

The fact that, in the literary tradition, the depiction of relatives is not at all connected with the circumstance of showing the breakdown of one and the same character is demonstrated by the traditional device of describing brothers— one noble, one criminal—but born into the same family.

Here everything, as is always the case in art, is the motivation of craftsmanship.

CONTEMPORARY THEATER

Embellished Tolstoy*

The First Distiller, written by Lev Tolstoy, embellished by Yury Annenkov—I am writing without the least bit of irony or admiration, simply stating a fact: the thing is bright and open in its composition.

Annenkov dealt with Tolstoy's text in the following way: he treated it as a scenario and expanded it by inserting accordion players, chastushki [folk poetry], a clown, acrobats, etc. These inserts are motivated in the following way: chastushki are inserted as songs sung by some peasants tipsy on some sort of "devilish swill"—accordion players and a round dance are also inserted into a scene of drunken revelry. The acrobats are presented as devils; that is, the circus is interpolated into the play as an illustration of hell. And finally the clown, in a red wig and wide "formal" pants, is presented without the slightest motivation. He simply came to himself redheaded and wandered into hell as into a café-chantant.

I'm not a reverential man and not respectful and on me the mixture of Tolstoy and cymbals, in and of itself, doesn't produce an irritating effect, but I would like to

---

*In the production at the Hermitage Theater of the artist Annenkov The First Distiller, written by Lev Tolstoy, Annenkov has interpolated new material into Tolstoy's text.

analyze this mixture, work out its essence and, mainly, attempt to understand what it can contribute.

Of course, the text of a work is not something untouchable, as was thought at the end of the nineteenth century and the beginning of the twentieth. In any case, we don't have the right to say that the freedom of dealing with someone else's text is a sign of "bad taste." Goethe reworked Shakespeare and a Shakespeare text itself consists of a stratification of all kinds, perhaps even reworkings by actors. Most of all, every reproduction of a work of art is a recreation, a restructuring, of its component parts, which is very clear if you scrutinize the copies made from one and the same work at a distance even, well, of twenty years. Annenkov's restructuring is good in that it does not imagine itself as a copy.

In art, the elaboration of the plot framework with material not organically connected with it is almost right. Let me remind you, for example, of the elaboration in *Don Quixote* where the plot is fleshed out by including virtually all the philosophical, didactic, folkloric, literary and even philosophical material of that time.

Sometimes such an elaboration is presented with motivation. Usually, though, it's threaded on speeches or on readings by the characters, as in Cervantes, Sterne, Goethe (*Werther*), Anatole France and hundreds of others.

Sometimes they're even presented on the principle of an intermezzo; that is, distinctive interpolations are inserted and concentrated in the roles of clowns or jokers, who don't take part in the basic action (if such there is) of the work.

In Shakespeare we encounter both methods of elaboration. Jokes, usually presented in the dialogue, are either pronounced by professional clown-specialists or are brought into the roles of the characters (*Much Ado about Nothing*). The same thing can be found in Molière. The conventionality of the motivation by the insertion of singing in vaudeville represents the same tendency. Such, too, is the role of "philosophical" interpolations in the psychological novel.

So the unexpectedness of Annenkov's interpolations is strictly superficial. It consists in the fact that the untouchable Tolstoy text is seemingly violated, though actually the framework underlying the elaboration of each adaptation of the work of art is always alien and, consequently, it would seem, untouchable. But, of course, that's not how it is. The Middle Ages developed the mystery play by closely relating its farcical material to the church service. Thus Annenkov, perhaps without entirely realizing it, turns out to be a force for the revival of tradition.

Of course, something eluded him. On the whole, the interrelations between "moralité" and farce don't come off. Let's see what the problem is. Drunken revelry and drunken singing—and sin in general, from the standpoint of "moralité"—are a sin, and are presented as such, but in the farce-bouffe it is amusing. These two planes do not differ sharply from one another, and the sinful plane is, of course, almost always purely "entertaining"—just as entertaining as Richardson's Lovelace was in the eyes of his female readers, but all the same the tendency is there, especially in Tolstoy. One doesn't have to take it into consideration, but for that one mustn't notice it. Annenkov noticed it.

The old man/grandfather, who is sitting during the interpolated scene, mumbles something about sin. These words, which I only partially heard, came across as follows: "The accordion players and the people are having a good time. Let them. It's not a sin . . ."

The fact that the old men are talking is not good. The action of the farce and the basic action should not interrupt one another; they should not get tangled up with one another. It's best not to lean against cardboard cliffs or to paint the frame of the picture in the same colors as the picture itself.

The mixture of farce and "moralité" interrupting one another and even trying to outdo one another—that's the main achievement of this jolly and talented production.

The ad-libbing of the red-haired man in checked trousers did not fill me with joy. It was too simply done. Annenkov inserted the following phrase into the play: "Anyuta, good-bye." And I, working along the same lines, will insert into my article the phrase: "My wife Zhenya and I are disappointed that we didn't see Yury Annenkov in the audience." It's very interesting to compare the production of *The First Distiller* with the Russian folk drama *Tsar Maximilian*. (I'm getting ready to write a separate piece about it, but I'll say this much: in Annenkov's production what dominates as material for articulation are the dance, the song and, mainly, the pantomime.) The result is a kind of mosaic. In folk drama, however, the basic text often washes away right down to the foundation and the "word" steps forward. Wordplay, puns—folk drama in that sense is a theater of the word.

Folk Comedy and The First Distiller

I really like the discussion that is enlivening the pages of *The Life of Art* on the question of Sergei Radlov's folk circus comedy.

In this discussion Mr. V. Soloviev and Mr. E. Kuznetsov insist that folk comedy is good, while Sergei Radlov asserts that it's exceedingly good.

I like Sergei Radlov's attitude toward what he's doing. I happen to think that much of what I'm doing is also good and significant.

Therefore I've decided to remind readers of my old article in *The Life of Art*. It's a review of Yury Annenkov's production of Lev Tolstoy's play *The First Distiller.*

Annenkov expanded this play with circus material and turned the whole thing into a circus scene—only then did conversations get started about a special "circus" troupe.

But between what Yury Annenkov was doing then and what Sergei Radlov is doing now in the Iron Hall of the People's House, there is a difference on which I want to linger. Annenkov, together with the circus, inserted into the play (formerly by Tolstoy) material of topical interest, chastushki, policemen in hell, etc. Radlov, as an epigone of the Italian comedy-improvisation, is attempting to use the action of comedy only as material for circus stunts.

Here he is making a big mistake. A degenerate circus tradition cannot provide material for improvisation since in fact improvisation always involves extracting old material from the general storehouse. True, Radlov thinks to found a studio in which he will train improvisation artists and stuff them with a batch of theater material.

But that's exactly like attempting to create a language on your own. A single-minded will can change a tradition but cannot create it. Annenkov's decision to proceed from material already in existence is more justified and, at the same time, more poignant.

Another characteristic differentiating trait in the two practitioners of "circus" comedy is that Annenkov chose to articulate a play having a pronounced plot. Radlov, however, frames his stunts with a rather weakly developed plot, in which there is almost no organizing core.

At the same time, Annenkov, as an artist of the new school, feels no need to motivate the interpolation of each artistic device. He introduced into his comedy characters completely disconnected from the plot. Thanks to this, for example, clown-Anyuta stood out much more vividly in the context of the basic plot than Radlov's parallel to the same device, the clown-messenger. It's interesting to observe that, like any innovator, Annenkov turned out to be a genuine connector of tradition. In the two planes, which are not amalgamated, the action takes place at the beginning of the development of European drama (in Aristophanes there is also such a duality) and in the Russian folk theater, as in the Turkish *Karagoz,* the elaboration of the material proceeds without motivation and the seams uniting the parts of the comedy are not painted over.

Annenkov and Radlov are linked by one general defect: theirs is a theater outside the word. Or, to be more exact, the word in it is in decline. In this is their failure and a sharp departure from folk art. As I have already written, in my note on *Tsar Maximilian (The Life of Art)* folk theater, especially the Russian variety, is not so much theater of movement in general as it is theater of a verbal dynamic. The word, the self-sufficient word, is dear to the people. Those involved with folk drama are no less masters of the word than the Futurist poets and modernists.

The factory chastushka also draws its life from the word, from wordplay and from the sense of the word.

Radlov descends directly from Yury Annenkov, laterally from Meyerhold's pantomimes. Here lies the explanation and the justification for their neglect of the word. Yury Annenkov's sin before the word is unforgivable.

My article is being printed in the same mode in which I myself exist—the discussion mode.

The Art of the Circus

Every art has its structure—that which transforms its material into something artistically experienced.

This structure finds its expression in various compositional devices: in rhythm, phonetics, syntax and plot. A device is something that transforms non-aesthetic material, imbuing it with form, into a work of art.

As far as the circus is concerned, things are going rather strangely. Its performances can be divided as follows: first, the farcical-theatrical section (with clowns); second, the acrobatic section; third, animal performances—artistically structured only in its first section.

Neither the snake man nor the strong man lifting heavy objects nor the bicyclist looping the loop, nor the animal trainer putting his well-pomaded head into the lion's jaws, nor the trainer's smile nor the lion's physiognomy—none of this is art and yet we perceive the circus as art, as no different from Annenkov's heroic theater.

It's interesting to trace the structure of the circus. What is its device? What distinguishes circus movement from everyday movement? Let's take the strong man and the animal trainer.

The scenes in which they participate are lacking a plot; therefore the circus can get along without a plot.

Their movements are not rhythmic; therefore the circus has no need of beauty.

Finally, all this is not even beautiful. As I write, I feel guilty for having used such an incomprehensible word as "beauty."

Thank God the circus has no need of beauty.

But in circus action there is always something common: circus action is difficult.

It is difficult to lift weights; it is difficult to bend like a snake; it is horrible, that is, also difficult, to put your head in a lion's jaws.

Without difficulty there is no circus; therefore, in the circus the artistic work of the acrobats under a dome is more artistic than the work of those acrobats in the parterre, though their movements were both in the first and in the second instances absolutely identical.

If the work were done without a safety net, it would be worse; it would partake of the circus more than if the work were made even slightly less dangerous by a net.

Making it difficult—that is the circus device. Therefore, if in the theater artificial things—cardboard chains and balls—were routine, the spectator at the circus would be justifiably indignant if it turned out that the weights being lifted by the strong man weighed less than what was written on the poster. Theater has other devices at its disposal than simple difficulty; therefore it can get along without it.

The circus is all about difficulty.

Circus difficulty is related to the general laws of breaking in composition.

Most of all, the circus device is about "difficulty" and "strangeness." One of the types of difficulty connected in literature with plot-breaking occurs when the hero, for example, gets himself into difficult situations through the struggle between the feeling of love and duty. An acrobat overcomes space with a leap, the animal trainer overcomes a wild beast with a glance, the weightlifter overcomes weight with strength, just as Orestes overcomes love for his mother in the name of rage for his father. And in this lies the kinship between heroic theater and the circus.

With Regard to Tastes

In France a questionnaire circulated as to who is the best playwright in the world.

An enormous majority of the votes went to Rostand. Shakespeare and Sophocles did not place.

In Shakespeare's time his theater was full, although perhaps not respected.

In Sophocles' time the theater was full and people probably knew what they were watching.

I have written this not to weep over some golden age and not to propose its revival on the spur of the moment.

Now the season is getting under way and the best theaters are opening with Shakespeare. It would be interesting to know how the public would respond to a questionnaire.

Is it normal to have a gap between the tastes of the public and the repertory? Is it necessary to educate the public? These days if we undertook to educate the public, we certainly wouldn't give it Shakespeare.

Rostand represents self-satisfied mediocrity, but veneration of the classics, restoration, is in my opinion also self-satisfied mediocrity.

For three years I've been waiting to see Blok's plays

performed on the stage. Mayakovsky's play was performed, then closed like a hostile flag treacherously raised over the fortress only to be immediately torn down.

Staging new plays in the big theaters is obviously a death sentence.

True, this general rule was violated with the production of Oks's *Masks*.

The good tastes of the Petrograd theaters do not fill me with joy.

That does not fill me with joy, nor do the shouts about the corruption of the language. Respectful shouts are very amusing. According to them, all of Russian literature ruined the Russian language, beginning with Tolstoy.

I know that the French, responding to the praise of Rostand, were at that time executioners of the Impressionists and are now bit by bit smothering everything vital in art. But even when the people attending Shakespeare's theater were told that "this is good," they insisted that it's not better than Rostand—that's a pillow in the face.

The opinion of the majority in art—it's all or nothing—art cannot be measured in that way. Classicism and good tone have never saved the day—especially today's museum, collegial classicism, repudiating nothing.

I, too, have no idea what to do with the theater.

I'm a man who wears under his tunic the yellow flag of the Futurists.

But I would like to see in place a theater of good taste and restoration—a theater which would be given the right to spoil art as it is now spoiling the language.

At least cinematography would be left without guardians and without historical films.

When the peasant in the folk tale started to make the weather, he did it very badly.

Now we are making art ourselves.

Apropos of King Lear

Unfortunately, at the moment I don't have even Shakespeare at hand and I'm not in a position to go looking for it, but, as is well known, many books, much like the lowest animals, can sometimes breed by germination, without fertilization.

The quantity of books that breed by germination includes a majority of the books about Shakespeare. One book leads to another and ten books produce an eleventh and so it goes with no letup in sight. This "booksickness" is unfortunately typical not just of the literature about Shakespeare. The sickness affects the whole history and theory of literature. In the recent past the whole field of the humanities was afflicted by it.

Therefore give me credit for not opening the library's floodgates at the start of this short article.

The least important thing about *King Lear,* in my opinion, is that the work is a tragedy.

Chekhov informed his friends that he had written a hilarious farce—*The Three Sisters*. Chekhov did not insert tears into his play.

Toward the end of his life, Gogol saw in his *Inspector-General* a tragedy and nothing else.

Yes, *The Inspector-General* can be interpreted as a tragedy and *The Three Sisters* can be staged by Smolyakov as a comedy.

Emotions and experiences are not the content of a work of art.

Hanslick, a theoretician of music, gives many examples of how one and the same piece of music can be interpreted now as sad, now as cheerful and witty.

In my opinion, I repeat, the content of *King Lear* is not the tragedy of a father but a series of situations, a series of witticisms, a series of devices organized so that they create by their interrelations new stylistic devices.

To put it simply, *King Lear* is a stylistic phenomenon.

Just as it is wrong to pasture cows on artificial grass, it is equally wrong to approach a work of art from a sociological or a psychological point of view.

People approaching works of art from such points of view always find in them that which is nonexistent, not fundamental—they always find in them a *type*.

In *King Lear* they also see a *type*.

A "type" is one of the inventions of non-scientific poetics. In art the artist always proceeds from the device conditioned by the material.

In Shakespeare's theater, the material consisted not only of the intrigue taking place on stage but also of puns— verbal games. For Shakespeare the verisimilitude of the type was of no importance. Why does Lear say one thing now and another later? Why do crude jokes simply pop into his mouth? For Shakespeare, King Lear is an actor, as actor and also a jester. But the jester is brought into the play precisely as a jester, though he is King Lear's jester, a fact that we don't always see in plays of a similar type. King Lear is brought into the work by a more private, personal motivation.

But Shakespeare's plays are situated in a period of developing devices for creating literature when motivation was still completely formal. (I'm not suggesting that devices get better as they replace one another.)

That's why the whole opening scene is so badly motivated and, in fact, its entire movement—in particular all those endless non-recognitions.

The speeches of King Lear are just as poorly connected to him as the speeches of Don Quixote about Hispanic literature are poorly connected to Alonzo the Good, who in his free time makes cages and toothpicks.

There are critics who think that one can make judgments about the behavior of the heroes in a work of art not on the foundation of the laws of art but on the foundation of the laws of psychology. These critics are, of course, interested in the question regarding the nature of King Lear's madness and are even looking for a suitable medical term in Latin.

It would be interesting to find out what disease the knight suffers from: after all, he always moves in an L-shaped manner.

How should King Lear be played?

He needs to be played not as a type. A type is a series of threads stitching the work together. A type is either a guide showing one landscape after another or else the motivation of effects.

One must act the play. One must bring out its material and not rely on a physiognomy that would explain its change.

King Lear must be played with emphasis on the punster and on the clown.

Lear's daughters are just as artificial as card damsels.

Cordelia is the trump card.

One would have to be blind not to feel in the play the conventionality of a folk tale and the intelligent hand of a connoisseur of theater.

The Old and the New

In *The Life of Art,* it's customary to see the new art being overthrown by Comrades E. Gollerbakh and Petr Storit-syn.

With such enemies you won't meet your maker soon.

Nowadays when all the talented people have gone out of Egypt and its cauldrons in order to seek new forms, when the old has grown as brittle as gum frozen with cocaine, it's amusing to read the following comment about Tatlin's counter-reliefs: "An abundance of such 'reliefs' may be encountered in cesspools, garbage dumps, old sheds and back alleys."

There are no limits to the naïveté of a country bump-kin: "The works of Strindberg, Tatlin, Kerev, Rozanov, Bruni, Malevich, Shkolnik, Baranov-Rossin and Lvov have all the trappings of a monumental misunderstanding."

One must talk about such people, who view even *The World of Art* as a misunderstanding, since one writes for the same newspaper as they.

Yesterday I was at the theater; yesterday I was at the student graduation spectacle performed by the Apollon Studio; yesterday there were no misunderstandings; yes-terday I was at the morgue.

There were a forest and a distant horizon and a tragic actor with an "R," saying "brrrrother," and an extremely fat woman moving her backbone in a way that was, in all probability, funny. The play proceeded without "misunderstandings."

No naïve heart, no brief artistic education leading to the ability to make extracts and quotations from *Bygone Years* (I can answer for my words and prove them, but I would be embarrassed).

Ostrovsky was being performed—and what kind of Ostrovsky! *It Gives off Light but No Heat.*

It was very academic and, perhaps, even governmental.

It was played according to the chik-chirik system—no serious mistakes but lots of twittering.

O, it's hard to keep looking, and the people kicking each other sometimes join forces to trample us with their flocks, but it would be better to die in the desert than to live as a corpse among corpses.

O, isn't it possible that our dead comrades could use their peculiar cold-bloodedness to speak at last about the seekers, though without attempts at wit?

How unaccustomed are the philistines to the fact that art is always before them, that those artists of interest to art history are only those who want to do something different from their predecessors. There are others, those who want to do the same thing over and over again, but they are of no interest.

By the way, this is from Brunetière.

Regarding Merezhkovsky

The Petersburg Drama Theater is preparing a production of dramas by Merezhkovsky and á la Merezhkovsky which will include: *Pavel*, *Alexander* and *Nicholas* (based on the novel *14 December*).

I stood in line a long time today and ran up and down the street, and therefore I almost can't write about literature without breaking the law against holding more than one job; I'm forced therefore to write approximately.

I don't want to emit a series of ringing curses, but the novels and dramas of Merezhkovsky give the impression of acting out Gypsy songs—some sort of dramatized historical joke.

Therefore the less we know about that epoch which Merezhkovsky is sketching for us, the more interesting are his works of art to us.

Here the entertainment value of the material wins us over. That is why the average reader gets more interested in *Julian the Apostate* and *Leonardo da Vinci* than in *Peter and Alexis*. To an individual familiar with the history of the Decembrists, *14 December* is boring and unpleasant with its device of summarizing badly chosen material, diluted by a mysticism which has already been standing too long.

14 December strikes me as a parody, something like Leonid Andreev's "The Fair Sabine Women," in which the Romans speak of themselves as "the ancient Romans." Merezhkovsky has the Decembrists interpret themselves from the point of view of a third-rate literary figure of the twentieth century.

It's interesting to compare the way Lev Tolstoy uses quotations in his works. Usually he has a "historical phrase" that appears in a certain context, that is, surrounded by words and situations that cause it to be perceived anew. Look, for example, at the conversation between Napoleon and Alexander's emissary.

Tolstoy creates the "historical phrase" anew and works it into the composition. Merezhkovsky pastes together phrases and verses into a sort of patchwork quilt.

I'm not criticizing Merezhkovsky for writing and pasting worse than Tolstoy. I'm simply pointing out that literary technique in Russia has developed in amazing ways during the last decade. Merezhkovsky's work, however, has degenerated into absolutely childish devices.

Merezhkovsky possesses yet another peculiarity: he is aging fast. One cannot listen to the poems he wrote at the beginning of his literary work without a feeling of awkwardness (example: "Sakya Muni").

Merezhkovsky's mysticism—his "Heaven Above," and "Heaven Below," "The Beast and God," "Christ and Antichrist"—all these words connected in pairs are worn out to the point where one cannot take them seriously.

I have no objection to the performance of Merezhkovsky on stage, but Merezhkovsky needs to be staged not on an artistic plane but on an educational one. His novels may be useful in the same way as his poems; therefore the attitude toward them should not be the same as toward whole works, as, for example, toward groups of sculptures and even not the same as toward whole suites, as, for example, toward suites of furniture, but as toward the connections of objects able to exist separately.

Mysticism—the bad mysticism of Merezhkovsky—should be sent into exile and scratched out of all his novels—not because it's mysticism but because it's bad mysticism.

I'm against the adaptation of Merezhkovsky's novel, but there's nothing to object to in the plays. These novels were not novels and they won't be dramas. In general, this is a profoundly non-literary phenomenon.

The Comic and the Tragic

What is interesting in the last production of the Theater of Folk Comedy is the alternation of comic and tragic moments.

The play is organized in the following way: its basic core consists of melodrama—the type represented by the penny dreadful, with its swift change of scenes, its catastrophic love affairs—in a word, its series of adventurous moments, connected almost without psychological motivation.

The play opens with the pantomime of a murder. The motivation of this murder is provided later with the help of a conversation.

The comic element is provided in the form of a clown, whose entrance into the play is motivated by the fact that he is a petit bourgeois on whose street the murder took place. He is fleeing to the provinces, but it turns out that he encounters criminals everywhere. In a word, he proves to be an accompaniment to the melodramatic action.

Now how is this comic element structured? The comic is presented here not as humorous words but as a clash of ordinary words with the antics of a clown. Thus the comic element is concentrated in the gesture and in the properties.

This is humorous and humorous in a theatrical way, but it seems to me that another type of humor is possible, one which is widely used in the circus: the clash between word and gesture. For example, one clown wants to jump over another and falls, saying, "There, I made the jump" (Bogatyrev).

In a more developed form, this becomes (on the material of the word) Dickens's joke: "If we're going, let's be off," said the parrot when the cat started dragging him around by the tail.

In any case, the humorous side of Sergei Radlov shows in him a man able to turn the alchemy of the theater into the chemistry of the theater by using the material consciously (scientifically).

But let's turn to the contrast between the comic and the tragic.

This device, when bared, is widely used in Russian choral songs of the type "Among the Level Valleys," with the refrain "Akh, you Sashka, my kanashka," etc.; moreover, the tempo and the rhythm change in the refrain. Change in the rhythm alone serves as the basis for the Russian folk song of the Upper Volga region, contaminated (formed) by the alternation of the songs of the chastushka and the long-drawn-out measure. Sometimes the contrast is presented right in the refrain, that is, the refrain is not only at odds with the text but carries within itself a contradiction. For example, after a humorous refrain, suddenly we hear the church refrain: "Have mercy upon us, Lord, have mercy upon us."

In that way the law of contrast can be observed among the most popular songs. It is only the demand of one literary style among many that makes it necessary to somehow justify the interpolation of such an element. To criticize Sergei Radlov for his failure to observe the verisimilitude of such an "interpolation" betrays a lack of understanding of these matters.

Incidentally, I want to bring Fielding into the discussion. He's an English writer of the eighteenth century from the ranks of the "realists" (in street terminology):

> And here we shall of necessity be led to open a new vein of knowledge which, if it hath been discovered, hath not to our remembrance been wrought on by any ancient or modern writer. This vein is no other than that of contrast.

This is followed by some examples. I'll cite the most relevant:

> A great genius among us will illustrate this matter fully. I cannot, indeed, range him under any general head of common artists, as he hath a title to be placed among those
>
> *Inventas qu vitam excoluere per artes.*
> Who by invented arts have life improved.
>
> I mean here the inventor of that most exquisite entertainment called the English Pantomime.
>
> This entertainment consisted of two parts, which the inventor distinguished by the names of the *serious*

and the *comic,* The serious exhibited a certain number of heathen gods and heroes, who were certainly the worst and dullest company into which an audience was ever introduced, and (which was a secret known to few) were actually intended so to be, in order to contrast the *comic* part of the entertainment, and to display the tricks of Harlequin to the better advantage.

The character of the tragic in Sergei Radlov's work partakes of the penny dreadful and I say this without reproach. The penny dreadful had an influence on Dostoevsky. Shakespeare was born not just in the Grand Dramatic Theater but also on the boulevard.

I've said any number of times that in the general course of literary history, the dominant can be created not by the resurrection of old patterns but by the canonization of the younger line in art.

Thus theoretically, Radlov is right.

Perhaps there was no need to repeat verbatim the forms of the American film, but it was necessary to use the framework of its structure.

Of the devices that connect the tragic and the comic in a play, particularly effective is the scene in which the thief and the detective change clothes. Changing clothes constantly into one new costume after another, they run around, stopped each time by the same question asked by the clown, and their answer reveals to the public that it's always the same people.

The text of the play is weak—to be more exact, not weak but missing altogether.

They say, but I don't know for sure, that film actors, while they're playing their parts, in order to facilitate the ideas of the mimic corresponding to a certain moment at a certain moment, utter "appropriate words." By means of such "appropriate words," subsidiary and artistically unorganized, the text, especially the text of a *tragic* play comes to life.

That is the fundamental mistake of Radlov and his theater. If the word were not necessary to the theater, one could stage a pantomime, but to speak on the stage "any old words" is just as criminal as to move "in any old way."

This must be said, though, if only out of respect for a brilliant production. Some of its moments—for example, the scene in which heads appear from behind all the projections, all the scenery—convey unexpectedness and inventiveness.

Sergei Radlov knows the theater well, but his knowledge overwhelms him.

The entire third act tumbles out of the play's plot.

Consequently, the play ends in the middle of itself.

This seems wrong to me since the first two acts are constructed not in Aristotle's way of interpolating episodes but by Aristotle's law of the single plot complicated by perepeteias.

Consequently, all sorts of familiar and unfamiliar stunts pile up in the third act: Clowns turn somersaults, policemen slide down slippery slides, Delvari cracks jokes. The only thing missing would be for Vladislav Khodasevich to come out on stage and, in the midst of this Sodom, begin to paint backdrops while Sergei Radlov reads his translation of Plautus's *Twins*.

I understand the joy of the inventor, overwhelmed with ideas, which are cavorting in his head, one after another, like a herd of sheep.

But just the same, seeing every possible stunt united in one place, I remembered that old anecdote about the high school student who wrote his composition without a single punctuation mark. Then he gathered all the marks that there are, putting all of them at the very end, and I want to end my article with that student's phrase: "Take your places."

Shoeing a Flea
(Toward the Question of Adaptations and Illustrations)

Leskov has a story called "Levsha."

The English gave Tsar Alexsander Pavlovich a steel flea that danced.

During the reign of Tsar Nicholas Pavlovich it was decided to put the English to shame. The flea was consigned to Tula. In Tula the flea was shod. Fine work—even under a microscope, it was impossible to sort out. The flea was sent abroad to dazzle foreigners.

The only problem was that the flea no longer danced. Every machine has its proportion and is calculated accordingly.

The English were indeed dazzled by the fine work, but they understood: People didn't know the multiplication tables.

I was attending a performance of Dickens's "The Cricket on the Hearth" at the first studio of the Moscow Art Theater.

As a recent refugee, I still lack the psychology of the sentry from Goncharov's *Oblomov*. That sentry ate the remnants of the master's Sunday meat pie on Thursday, enjoying the thought that the meat pie was seigniorial.

I've forgotten his name—Ofrosimov, I think.

I didn't like the performance. The play was done with astonishing subtlety. Chekhov, to speak very seriously, is a great actor. Giatsintova did a good job. The reader Nevsky read badly.

But I'm not writing reviews. I know one thing and about one thing I'm certain. It's impossible to shoe a flea.

It's impossible to dramatize a short story.

It is necessary to know the multiplication tables and to remember that everything is calculated according to its proportion.

A very nice short story was made into an unbearable play.

I viewed the stage with interest.

Two people were chatting; the rest had nothing to do.

The director was experienced. He hid them behind a stove. Or sent them up a ladder.

But throughout the whole performance you felt the strain; you felt that the actors were playing something that was impossible to play. A sedentary play. In Dickens almost everything is built on the device of the riddle. In great works one riddle, having been solved, is replaced by another.

A riddle (a stranger) provides the structure of "The Cricket on the Hearth." But Dickens's solutions are not at all theatrical. They are inactive to such a degree that the novelist (usually) needs to finish his work with a story explaining the mystery. That's how the following novels end: *Nicholas Nickleby, Martin Chuzzlewit, Our Mutual Friend, Little Dorrit.* "Cricket" ends in the same way. This is not an elaboration of the action. This is its slow twist and semi-satisfying explanation at the end.

Short stories and novellas are made not just with the help of words: They're made out of words and by the law of the word. It's impossible to translate a work of art from one material to another. When Masiutin illustrated Gogol's "The Nose," the thing simply disappeared because the entire structure of the tale lay in its irony. Now the nose travels in its stagecoach, wearing the uniform of a court councilor. Now it is wrapped in a small rag and baked in the bread.

Gogol deliberately combines both moments.

A police officer brings the major his nose, which is real, though cut off, and reports that he caught it in the image of a man.

Gogol was an extremely daring writer who was published in his own time only because the general level of literary understanding then was higher than it is now. The situation called for absurdity. In the last redaction of "The Nose" Gogol rejected the suggestion to motivate the absurdity with a dream. What he needed was a pure form.

Gogol's book with Masiutin's illustrations (the Helicon edition) is a big and marvelously shod flea.

The beginning of Dickens's tale—this conversation between the narrator and the reader as to who came first, the teapot or the cricket—is a game with reality, a game in which, of course, no one but the author knows who tuned up first, About this device, about its reason I could say a lot. But let's return to the theater. It's quiet. The curtain dangles. The sound of the boiling teapot reverberates; then, in about five minutes the cricket tunes up. Then the reader comes out and argues about something that was clear to the whole theater: "The teapot got a head start."

The text seems to have been preserved, but in fact, it turns senseless.

Don't get the idea that I'm speaking about insignificant details. I'm speaking about the structure of the thing.

One can discard from a thing elements of its form, but, even if you tear all the leaves off a head of cabbage, the head will remain.

Neither Russian art nor the First Studio of the Moscow Art Theater needs to be patronized. Let's measure one another with a full measure.

Everything has its arithmetic. "Cricket" has been carrying on an illegal existence for nine years.

Let those who nibble on a stale pie not take offense.

Eating Fish by Cutting It with a Knife . . .

. . . is forbidden——and not because it's improper (what's that to us?) but because the instrument is not suitable.

The flesh is soft——impossible to cut.

Therefore I haven't written about Evreinov.

I've kept silent for a long time, and very well, too. On the whole, it's good to keep silent in the presence of those who will be speaking and we have learned to keep silent brilliantly.

Posters are hanging everywhere: "More Important," "Most Important," "Most Important of All!!"

And they've been hanging long enough: I'm going to write.

But first I'm going to change the heading.

Now we're proceeding with a new heading.

A Thousand Herrings

There are books of mathematical problems; the problems in them are arranged in order. Some problems concern an equation with one unknown. A bit farther on are problems concerning the quadratic equation.

The answers are found at the back of the book. They are given as an even column, in order:

4835	5 sheep
4836	17 cranes
4837	13 days
4838	1000 herring

Woe betide him who begins the study of mathematics directly from the "answers" and tries to make sense of that exact column.

The problems are important and the course of their solutions—not the answers.

Those theoreticians whose interest in works of art confines itself to the ideas, the conclusions, and not the structure of things, find themselves in the position of a man who, wanting to study mathematics, studies the columns of answers.

Their heads are filled with the following charts:

The romantics = renunciation of religion
Dostoevsky = the God-seeking movement
Rozanov = the gender question
The year '18 = renunciation of religion
The year '19 = the God-seeking movement
The year '20 = the sexual question
The year '21 = resettlement in Siberia

But for the theoreticians of art, fish-smoking factories have been set up at the universities. That way they don't disturb anyone.

Unfortunate is the writer who tries to augment the weight of his work not by articulating its direction but by magnifying the "answer" to his problem.

As if problem No. 4837 were bigger and more important than problem No. 4838 because the answer to the former is given as 13, and the answer to the latter as "a thousand herrings."

It's simply a case of two problems, both intended for the third class of the gymnasium.

Evreinov's *The Most Important* is a vaudeville with an enormous answer.

Something vaguely similar to Jerome Jerome's "The Passing of the Third Floor Back" is mixed in with Rychalov's *Tour*. Add a few postcard Christs and you get something very bad, though rather theatrical . . . but I'm mistaken about the genre. The result is a mediocre vaudeville.

O, don't frighten us with the Paraclete. Don't comfort us with Dr. Fregoli. Don't level all of this out with a harlequinade.

No force brought from the outside into a work of art can strengthen it except the structure of the work itself.*

If those sitting in the theater were blessed with wit, the ceiling would crack from the guffaws over the idea that a man, in order to gain access to a stage, would go to such lengths as to write a play, one more play.

Poor Evreinov! Such a big response to such a trivial action.

P.S. For the sake of compactness, I will insert a book review here.

The other day a book came out by a man whose name I will not mention in order to deprive him of free publicity.

Let's choose a name at random——Mr. Y.

The book was wonderfully produced on eighty-pound paper.

Preface by Evreinov, drawings by Annenkov.

What pleases Evreinov about Mr. Y is understandable. Mr. Y. is a boundary toward which Evreinov is striving.

I was unpleasantly surprised to find Annenkov's name in that book. What's more, his drawings in it are not completely appropriate.

But there are all sorts of names—a regular jumble.

Here's one more: Viktor Shklovsky.

---

*Meyerhold, whom I dislike, has created a school for directors interested in mastery of the scene. He has at least created technicians. Evreinov has created nothing in art; he has simply applied some face powder to the old theater.

COMPLETING THE FRAME

I and My Coat

The ceiling is solid; very solid is the ceiling.

―――――

I was given a locomotive the size of my writing desk, but you don't know the size of my writing desk.

It is no secret that such locomotives were very few in Russia; in Russia there are, on the whole, very few locomotives. I never traveled on locomotives; that is, I never served as an engineer on one, but I did actually ride on one just once in the Ukraine on a tender, above the coal. The tender was small. I moved the handle from the side (as you engage a gear in an automobile) and I set out with some eight young people.

We rode standing up and were higher than the engine's smokestack. Then we stopped and looked to see what was the matter. We opened (very easily) the inside of the engine and it was the same as that of a four-cylinder automobile.

Except that this one didn't work. The white, clean, silver washtub of the crankcase and the bent crankshaft, slightly more gray than the crankcase, and the connecting rods, like arms, clasping the curves of the shaft with the palms of the bearings. Palms, yes, but damaged. Meanwhile, the pistons, like putrid water, are pumping out into a motley hue, and the piston rings are twisted.

The piston rings in the piston were twisted and the piston itself was bent upward.

The metal was torn apart in an inhuman way. The way a shell fragment, understanding nothing, cuts a strip on a man's body.

And everything had been damaged, damaged beyond repair. The engine was wrecked. They don't run very well without oil.

Shame pummeled me from above on the shoulders. "This is industrial propaganda! We've only had locomotives in Russia for fifty years, only fifty." It was wrong to put quotation marks around the phrase. They should have been put around the whole story. It's shameful in the same way as if a doctor were giving me a checkup and I were sitting naked in the gynecological chair. To my right is the entire "House of Arts" and to my left is the entire "House of Literary Scholars." The hairs on my whole body are standing on end from shame.

I wrecked the locomotive by running it without oil. Why did I say say that I knew how to do it?

I was taken to court—a revolutionary court. "Defendant," I was asked, "why did you wreck the locomotive?"

I am totally speechless. I am guilty, guilty to the core.

Even my blood is guilty.

But after all, don't I have to say something?

I decided to wake up. But I was ashamed to wake up.

After all, I had literally wrecked the engine by not checking the oil. I didn't have the right to wake up.

Like insulting a woman and then discarding her.

Is it really possible to be so confused, to be so overwhelmed with guilt and then to run away and wake up?

It's shameful to say so, but I did wake up.

This was shame and it rejected me.

I floated out of sleep through the ceiling.

My wife was beside me.

She didn't know how guilty I was, so she kept sleeping.

And the ceiling was solid over me, like bone.

———

Like air with raindrops, life is permeated with other lives, other worlds.

One wheel is turning and intersecting with another wheel. The machine is working in another machine.

This cannot be, yet it is. You know it yourself.

Twisted into another world, my wife lies there and sleeps, not knowing that I have committed an offense in a third world.

Our life is being woven on a strange loom. The threads in it crisscross.

When the fabric is taken from the loom, we see something strange: not the fabric and not something resembling a bridge and not something resembling an airplane, but a wheel working where there is already a wheel working at a different angle, like life, pierced by other lives, like air pierced by rain.

Perhaps our life itself is like rain piercing another life.

Solid is the ceiling over my head.

———

I jumped out of "there," but not completely. Perhaps I stayed there.

I am there, yet my coat and my felt boots are here, taking a walk, and that is why my coat and slippers are so roomy.

This is making me sick to my stomach. I feel like throwing up.

And it's not true that I'm here and that on the day after tomorrow I will be invited to edit a humorous journal, *The Free Corpse*.

Yesterday evening, on Volodarsky Street, next to Building 46, not far from Basseiny, I met my coat and my felt boots.

They were tap dancing.

In a rather restrained way.

But how unconstructive—a tap dance in felt boots.

That's not logical.

A tap dance needs to be tapped out.

I know why my coat and my felt boots have absolved themselves of me, just as I absolve myself of responsibility for this story and I know why they weren't dancing the cancan.

They were afraid to let on that they had no knees.

I stood in front of them and looked.

In the same way, no doubt, that the "I," discarded by me in sleep, was tormented.

At this point out crawled the devil in full regalia and began to look both at me and at my boots.

But the devil landed here by chance. He had escaped from one of Remizov's stories. I take no responsibility for his actions.

All the same, my coat looks like me. For example, it can dance, though badly, but it can't stand around in its shirt-sleeves, with its collar hanging down, and therefore Sergei Radlov will not accept it into his theater "Folk Comedy."

The ceiling is solid.

———

Don't kill me out of pity. I'm not suffering terribly. So a traveler saw in the desert a man who had shoved his foot in his mouth. He said to him, "Why are you eating your foot?"

And the man replied, "I'm not eating it: I'm washing it."

Don't kill me. Save the shipping expenses.

Don't hold me by these . . . I don't know what they're called . . . Don't hold me by these arms.

Do you think I want to bob to the surface?

Wife, you surely don't want me to desert you?

And why then are you going away from me into your own dream?

In the sky curve the broken piston rings.

There's no oil at the bottom of Petersburg.

Hold fast to the stacked paws of the crankshaft bent by the effort of pulling out the crankshaft.

The ceiling is solid over my head.

I'm sick of my coat.

Let go of my arms. I won't bob to the surface. All I want to do is write a New Year's story.

31 December 1920

A ROCK ON A STRING

Rollercoaster

What a strange thing a newspaper is.

In general, the organization of human souls—not the inside of an individual soul but the structure of souls, their range—that is a strange business.

———

At the corner of the Neva and the canal marking off the Fortress of Peter and Paul from the Petrograd side of town, or at the corner of the canal by which the Neva fastens the fortress to itself . . .

It's the very same corner.

A couple of words about the fortress. When you write about it, its spire is so deeply etched in the memory and so many memories everywhere, on all sides, that they run around it like the road to Djulfa around Mt. Ararat and you want to write the words Peter and Paul from the bottom up, using the spire as a pen.

But I'm not going to write.

Sometime, for example, I want to publish an article diagonally in the newspaper and apparently the reason here is not architecture alone.

———

Now, having specified the spot, I can say that at this very spot (on the corner of the canal) stands a badly made mountain with two peaks.

———

The mountain functions from four to twelve.

On it run little cars: apparently two. I often see two at once when I look at the mountain from Palace Bridge or from the Stock Exchange Bridge.

In a day the little cars make a specific number of circuits and a specific number fall down the tracks and fly down the steep slope.

The heart stops beating.

And the number of times designated by the builder of the mountain people shout in the car:

A-a-a . . . akh! . . . a-a-a-a-akh!

It's a squeal factory.

O, dear comrades from the newspapers of the whole world, what a strange business is a newspaper.

What a terrible thing is an organization of souls.

We will be writing at some other time. Our hearts will break.

I don't want to slander the heart.

Together we will publish our articles and we will shout all together:

I want to break rank.

Coffins Back

I happened to be going from the Ukraine to Russia with prisoners of war. It must have been 1918.

I wasn't escorting them—I was traveling with them. I was dressed like them and, like them, I was cold.

I was making my way back to Russia.

We were not dressed for the occasion. In our wooden clogs, we were freezing on the floor of freight cars. The stoves had been ripped out of them.

Coming toward us in trains packed to the ceiling with flour, the Germans were pillaging the Ukraine.

We were freezing in trains abandoned along the way.

We were going on foot, wrapped in rags, stepping on railroad ties and pounding on them with our clogs, wood on wood.

We traveled by night. Petlyura's men, Germans, Bolsheviks—they all allowed us to cross the border.

We moved separately, like a current in the midst of the sea.

A cold current.

In the morning we woke one another up, but not everyone would wake up.

We were traveling across Russia.

Traveling with us in certain trains, on platforms, were coffins.

On the coffins was scrawled in black letters: **COFFINS BACK**

The dead were buried near Kursk in a "scorched forest."

And I kept walking with everyone. I can lose myself in a crowd and not feel unhappy by myself.

So we returned, the first prisoners of war from Germany—not from "civilian jobs," but from factories and mines.

That's what I remembered when I heard that the Upper Volga Region, dislodged by famine, had set off, leaving behind the "scorched fields"—set off, some to the north, some to the south and some to the Indian tsar.

A Boxer Down for the Count

The spirit is flagging.

We are smashed to pieces.

Life is not built by us.

I was in such despair that if I were to cross my legs, I wouldn't know which of them was the right leg, which the left.

We're like the family of barons from Andreev's play *That One*. All the males in the family are impotent, but the breed continues.

Every morning someone gets out of my bed and climbs into my pants and notices that the pants are too short for him.

But whether it's the same man every time—I have no idea.

Right now I'm lying firmly in a soft lead pipe under the ground.

Water is running through me.

Is it possible that I am just a tube through which time runs?

I have lost myself.

This is part of a play. I can't get it produced.

———

Like a boxer who's down for the count, I'm lying in the sand and feeling with my body the grating cold.

Someone is counting the seconds over me: one . . . two . . . three . . . four . . . If I don't get up by the count of "ten," I'm done for.

The Spire of the Cathedral of St Peter and St. Paul

I heard it in the freight car for prisoners of war.

Some of our soldiers so grieved in captivity that they had stopped washing themselves and were covered with lice and had even stopped talking.

The Germans were ruthless. They ordered that such people be scrubbed with hard brushes and washed in cold water.

Citizens, it's forbidden to laugh.

Citizens, it's forbidden to cry.

One must feel their connection with the state.

One must get back the will to live.

Just as the train on the Djulfa road always runs around Ararat, so a rock goes around on a string and cannot leave it, as the Neva cannot leave Petersburg, so I cannot leave Russia.

> And the decorated spokes
> get stuck in muddy ruts . . .
> —Aleksandr Blok

A Free Port

The agreements, which have
already given us herring
—Radek

Not true, no. Not the whole truth. Not even a fourth of the truth.

I don't dare to speak for fear of awakening the soul. I put it to sleep and covered it with a book so that it could hear nothing.

———

The Nicholas Station harbors a gravestone. A clay horse stands there, with its legs apart; it stands beneath the clay bottom of a clay policeman. They look like they are made of bronze. Over them is a wooden sign, "Monument to Freedom." Four tall masts stand at the street corners.

Some urchins peddle "Zephyir 300" for those who need a cigarette, but when the police come with their rifles to catch them and haul them off to an orphanage for children, where their souls would be saved, the urchins would shout "Scram!" and, whistling professionally, would run in all directions, ending up at the "Monument of Freedom."

Then they would lie low in that strange place—in the

void beneath the planks that separate Tsar Alexander III from the revolution.

But when the "shepherds" came with their rifles, they weren't looking for lost sheep. The children, as in a game of tetherball, would swing on the long ropes hanging from the masts on the corner.

I used to be cheerful. I'm sorry that I'm not my former self. If I were, I would take a brush and some black paint and I would write on this wooden sign of the Petersburg Gavroches:

> ## CHILDREN'S HOME

At the Stock Exchange Bridge, people would spend the whole day on narrow rafts, floating on the water, probing the bottom with boathooks, looking for wood that had sunk years before.

So a man having no dinner picks his teeth.

———

People are fishing on the bridges. One man stands and casts. About ten men are watching. The fish are not biting.

The salmon have emigrated. They cast their lot with the Estonians.

Small fish are being caught.

When Nevsky Prospekt was the Neva, those little fish were called *kolyushki*. I don't know what they're called now that Nevsky Prospekt is called Prospekt of October 25.

———

On Goncharovaya 14, a house cracked open and came tumbling down. A four-story one. It was undermined by the flooding of the basement. It settled like a top hat.

I've never seen a top hat.

The only smokestack which is still smoking over Petersburg is the water tower.

Both day and night the water tower pumps water from the Neva. The broken pipes flow into the basements and the water undermines the foundation.

———

Petersburg smells of space and sea.

The grass is green in the streets.

All around the city are vegetable gardens . . . as far as the eye can see . . .

Those who don't want to die work the land.

Not everyone wants to die.

The city has been stripped of its urban features.

At the corner of Vvedensky and Kronverk streets, people are plowing.

Instead of burned fences and buildings, new fences have been built of old rusty iron—new fences.

The houses had been torn down for firewood. The empty lots resemble the fields of Finland, where people make piles of bricks and broken toilets. From the bricks they make fences like those seen in the fields of Finland. But most of the time the new fences are made of old iron.

———

Cafés have opened on the streets. The store windows display rolls, fillet of sturgeon, sugar. At first, people just stood there and gawked. Now they keep walking.

———

In the Summer Garden (in the pond and in the Moika Canal at the Field of Mars) people are swimming (mostly children).

The linden trees there are enormous.

A paradise, lost and then regained.

———

That's not the whole truth, nor even one-fourth of the truth. I don't want to remember.

What a strange country.

Where everyone supplies his own transportation, where everyone serves as his own gardener, where everyone makes his own boots.

In Kazan they harness camels to the streetcars.

A country of electrification and Robinson Crusoes.

A F T E R W O R D

The Tsar's Kitchen

I sat and I laughed,
Because of a folk tale.

A certain tsar was powerful. A thousand camels carried
his kitchen, another thousand carried the supplies for his
kitchen, yet another thousand carried his cooks.

There was a war and the tsar was defeated.

He languished in captivity, in strong fetters.

He ate from a pot.

A dog ran by, knocked over the pot, got itself tangled in
the handle and carried the pot home.

The tsar began to laugh.

The guard asked, "Why are you laughing?"

The tsar said: "A thousand camels carried my kitchen,
another thousand carried the supplies for my kitchen, yet
another thousand carried the cooks. And now a dog has
carried away my kitchen on its tail."

———

I sat and I laughed.

In 1917 I wanted happiness for Russia. In 1918, I wanted
happiness for the whole world—wouldn't settle for less.
Now I want just one thing: to return to Russia.

This is the end of the knight's move.
The knight turns its head and laughs.

Translator's Notes

The following are annotations of names/terms used by Shklovsky that may not be familiar to an American reader.

Altman, Nathan (1889-1970): Painter who worked in a Cubist style. He organized the Cubist and Futurist decorations in Petrograd to celebrate the first anniversary of the revolution. He became director of the Petrograd section of the Department of Fine Arts.

Andreev, Leonid (1871-1919): Author of gloomy plays and short stories.

Annenkov, Yury (1889-1974): Pseudonym of Boris Temiryazov. Painter, theater designer, graphic artist, memoirist.

Awl: Reference to an old saying that a soldier "can shave with an awl."

Bazhenov, Vasily (1737-1799): Outstanding Russian architect of the Gothic revival.

Bebutov, Valery M. (1885-1961): Bebutov and Meyerhold co-directed a revolutionary production of Verhaeren's play *Dawns*. The premiere took place in November, 1920.

Belinsky, Vissarion (1811-1848): Critic, proponent of Russian realism. Described by Shklovsky as the "killer of Russian literature."

Bely, Andrei (1880-1934): Pseudonym of Boris N. Bugaev. Primary Symbolist poet, novelist, and theoretician.

Blok, Aleksandr (1880-1921): Primary Symbolist poet. The line on which Blok's discussion of the word *railroad* is based is as follows: "The anguish of rail, of road, whistled by, rending her heart."

Bogatyrev, Petr G. (1893-1971): Folklorist and literary scholar.

Browning: A type of pistol distributed before the Revolution to members of the Party or the Cheka as a reward for services rendered. Those who got their pistols first had the smallest numbers. A man unfriendly to Shklovsky attended a masquerade at the House of Arts, after which he published a denunciation of the event under the pseudonym of "Browning No.——" to suggest that he was a hero of the Revolution. Shklovsky, as usual, had the last word, indicating that he had such a high number that he'd probably got involved with the Party well after the fighting was over.

Brunetière, Ferdinand (1849-1906): French literary critic.

Ceiling: In the English translation of *A Sentimental Journey*, p. 242, Shklovsky recalls the night he fled from his Petersburg apartment to escape arrest—March 4, 1922—and says, "Just before that, I dreamed that the ceiling was falling on me."

Chateaubriand, Francois-Auguste-Rene (1768-1848): French author and diplomat, the preeminent literary figure in the France of his day.

Chekan, Victoria (1888-1974): Co-author of the play *Legend of a Communard*; cf. Mgebrov.

Chukovsky, Kornei (1882-1969): Pseudonym of Nikolai V. Korneichukov. Literary critic, writer for children, known for his monograph on Nekrasov and for his translations of Walt Whitman.

Chulkov, Georgy I. (1879-1939): Writer and critic.

Delacroix, Ferdinand (1798-1863): French historical painter.

Delvari, George: Famous clown known as Anyuta. In 1920 he worked in the Theater of the People's Comedy.

Derzhavin, Nikolai S. (1877-1953): Literary historian.

Dumas *père*, Alexandre (1802-1870): One of the most popular French writers of the nineteenth century.

Erckmann-Chatrian: Pseudonym of Emile Ekmann (1822-1899) and Alexandre Chatzian (1826-1890). Two of the first French regionalist novelists of the nineteenth century.

Evreinov, Nikolai. (1879-1953): Playwright and director, historian and theorist of the theater. Reacted against the realism prevalent in turn-of-the-century Russian theater.

Fielding, Henry (1707-1754): Novelist and playwright. One of the founders of the English novel. I'm indebted to Professor Martin Battestin for the information that the passages quoted by Shklovsky are to be found in book five, chapter one, of *Tom Jones*. Professor Battestin also pointed out that the reference to a "great genius" is ironic. Fielding is mocking John Rich, famous in pantomime as Harlequin.

France, Anatole (1844-1924): Pseudonym of Jacques Anatole Thibault. Satirist, novelist, and critic.

Fregoli, Leopold (1867-1936): Italian artist famous for his skill as a quick-change artist

Futurism: The Futurist movement was a dominant trend of the years 1910-1930. It began as a revolt against both Russian Realism (1830-1880) and Russian Symbolism (1890-1910). These artists rejected the role of the artist as photographer. They wanted to distort reality, to break the object into its components, and then to rearrange the components. Experimentation spread through all the arts: painting, photography, prose, poetry, film, music, dance. The movement was crushed in the late twenties when Stalin asserted Party control over industry, agriculture—and art.

Gavroche: A street urchin in Victor Hugo's *Les Miserables*. He dies a hero on the barricades.

Ginzburg, Ilya (1859-1939): Sculptor with whom Shklovsky studied.

Giotto (1266-1387): Giotto di Bondone, Florentine painter and architect.

Gogol, Nikolai (1809-1852): Russian novelist, satirist.

Gollerbach, E. (1895-1942): Art critic.

Goncharov, Ivan (1812-1891): Russian novelist.

Gorchakov, Nikolai (1898-1958): *The Theater in Soviet Russia* (New York, 1957), p. 60.

Gornfeld, Arkady G. (1867-1941): Literary historian.

Hanslick, Eduard (1825-1904): Austrian music critic.

Helmholtz, Herman L. (1821-1894): German physicist, mathematician, physiologist and psychologist.

Hildebrandt, Adolf (1847-1921): German sculptor.

Hitopadesa (Salutary Advice): Masterpiece of Sanskrit literature. Animal fables.

Hoffmann, E. T. A. (1776-1822): Writer, painter, musician.

Jerome, Jerome K. (1859-1927): English novelist and playwright.

Kerzhentsev (1881-1940): Pseudonym for Platon Mikhailovich Lebedev. Active in Bolshevik party from the beginning. Served as deputy director of *Izvvestiya* and manager of ROSTA. He eventually became ambassador to Sweden and to Italy.

Khlebnikov, Velimir V. (1885-1922): Leader of the Futurist movement. Shklovsky's piece refers to Khlebnikov's manifesto "The Trumpet of the Martians," in which he declares his contempt for the philistines and his intention to withdraw the Futurists from their society and to declare them Martians.

Khodasevich, Vladislav (1886-1939): Poet and critic.

Kruchenykh, Aleksei (1886-1968): Futurist poet and literary theorist.

Leontiev, K. (1831-1891): A brilliant literary critic, known especially for his work on Tolstoy.

Leskov, N. S. (1831-1895): Pseudonym for Stebnitsky, novelist and short-story writer.

Livy, Titus (59 B.C.-A.D. 17): Roman historian.

Lunacharsky, Anatoly (1875-1933): First Soviet commissar for education.

Lunts, Lev and Nikolai Nikitin: Both Lunts and Nikitin were members of the Serapion Brothers, a group of ten young people who had experienced world war, revolution and civil war. They were eager to convert their experiences into literature. Three outstanding established writers agreed to meet with the students every Saturday and to critique the prose that they produced. The three writers were Maksim Gorky, Viktor Shklovsky and Evgeny Zamyatin.

Konstantin Fedin, who wrote the review of *Knight's Move*, discussed at the end of my introduction, was also a Serapion. He was most closely aligned with Gorky and tried hard, without much success, to avoid Shklovsky's influence. See my article "Shklovsky, Gorky, and the Serapion Brothers" in *SEEJ* 12, no. 1 (1968).

Malevich, Kazimir (1878-1935): Created Suprematism, the first school of abstract painting in Russia.

Mayakovsky, Vladimir (1893-1930): Leading poet of the Russian avant-garde.

Merezhkovsky, Dmitry (1865-1941): Russian poet and novelist.

Meyerhold, Vsevolod (1874-1940): Highly influential avant-garde director.

Mgebrov, Aleksandr (1884-1966): Actor, director, founder of the Theater of the Proletkult in Petersburg in 1918. Co-author of the play *Legend of a Communard*.

Mystery-Bouffe: In his book *Meyerhold the Director*, Konstantin Rudnitsky makes the following statement: "*Mystery-Bouffe* was the first fully and thoroughly political play in the history of Russian theater. It was a play without love, without psychology, without plot in the previous traditional sense." The premiere was on November 7, 1918. The decorator for the staging was the Suprematist K. Malevich. The directors were Meyerhold and Mayakovsky.

Nadkin the Telegrapher: A character invented by the humorist Arkady Averchenko (1882-1925).

Ostrovsky, A. N. (1823-1886): Russian playwright.

Petlyura, Simon (1879-1926): Ukrainian nationalist leader. After the Polish-Russian Treaty of Riga, which left the Ukraine under the control of the Soviets, he emigrated to France, where an assassin shot him in retaliation for the pogroms committed by his army.

Piotrovsky, Adrian (1898-1942): Critic and journalist.

PROLETKULT: Organization for Proletarian Culture. Founded in 1906, it became important after the October Revolution when it pressed claims to having its own class, independent even of the Party. Lenin put a stop to these claims and forced it to be subservient to NARKOMPROS, but the idea of a separate proletarian culture persisted in the doctrines of Socialist Realism.

Puni (Pougny), Ivan (1894-1956): Painter who emigrated in l920 and who settled in Paris, where he adopted the French version of his name.

Quarenghi, Giacomo (1744-1817): Italian architect who belonged to the classical school. He designed the Academy of Sciences, the Smolny Institute and the Alexander Palace in Tsarskoe Selo.

Rastrelli, Bartolomeo (1700-1771): Italian architect who designed, among other buildings, the Hermitage, the Smolny Convent, and the Catherine Palace in Tsarskoe Selo.

Remizov, Aleksei (1877-1957): Symbolist writer.

Repin, Ilya (1844-1930): Russian painter, member of the Wanderers.

Ribot, Theodule (1839-1916): French psychologist.

Richardson, Samuel (1689-1761): English novelist.

Rodin, Auguste (1840-1917): French sculptor.

Roland (Orlando): hero of the Charlemagne epic.

ROSTA (Rossiskoe Telegrafnoe Agentstvo): Russian Telegraphic News Agency.

Rybnikov, Pavel (1831-1885): Philosopher, ethnologist.

Sardou, Victorien (1831-1908): Popular French playwright during the late nineteenth century.

Schiller, Johann (1759-1805): German dramatist.

Serednyak: a peasant neither rich nor poor but somewhere in the middle.

Smolyakov, L.: Comic actor and producer.

SOVNARKOM (Sovetsky Narodny komisariat): Soviet People's Commissariat.

Tatlin, Vladimir (1885-1953): Founder of the school of Constructivism. His Monument to the Third International was never built, but the maquette is stored in the Russian Museum in St. Petersburg.

Teffi, Nadezhda (1872-1952): pseudonym of Nadezhda Buchinskaya. Writer and poet.

Telegrafistka, Nadkin: Character invented by the humorist Averchenko.

THIRD INTERNATIONAL: Founded in March, 1919, to deal with the situation in Europe, where the revolutionary mood of the people was being thwarted by their leaders. Lenin believed that the Soviet state would not survive without other revolutions in Europe.

Thomon, Thomas de (1754-1813): Swiss architect who designed the ensemble containing the Rostral Columns in St. Petersburg.

Trotsky, Lev: "The Formalist School of Poetry and Marxism," in *Literature and Revolution* (Ann Arbor, 1960), p. 60.

Vampuka, The African Princess: A parody opera written by V. G. Erenburg and M. N. Volkonsky. First performed in St. Petersburg in 1900.

Vengerov, Semen (1885-1920): Scholar who viewed literature as an integral part of socio-historical developments.

Veronese, Paolo (1528-1588): Italian painter of the Venetian school.

Veselovsky, Aleksandr (1838-1906): Philologist

Wanderers: A group of artists who broke away from the powerful Petersburg Academy of Arts in 1863. They wanted to transform Russian culture by setting up exhibitions in the countryside, idealizing the peasant and his craft.

Wundt, Wilhelm (1832-1920): German psychologist and physiologist.

Yudenich, General Nikolai (1862-1933): After the October Revolution, he took command of the White Army in the Baltic area, from which he launched the attack on Petrograd in October 1919.

Zhirmunsky, Viktor (1891-1971): Literary scholar.

Acknowledgements

I want to thank Martin Battestin and James Heffernan
for their help with the Fielding material. I also want to
thank my new friend and colleague Misha Gronas, who
frequently came to the rescue when difficulties arose.
And, of course, my wife Karen and my dear friend Martha
Manheim, for their patience and encouragement. Finally,
I want to acknowledge an enormous debt to my long-time
friend and colleague Lev Loseff, who spent prodigious
amounts of time reading the manuscript from stem to
stern and making invaluable suggestions.

Richard Sheldon
Dartmouth College
Hanover, New Hampshire
May 2005

SELECTED DALKEY ARCHIVE PAPERBACKS

FOR A FULL LIST OF PUBLICATIONS, VISIT:
www.dalkeyarchive.com

SELECTED DALKEY ARCHIVE PAPERBACKS

FOR A FULL LIST OF PUBLICATIONS, VISIT:

www.dalkeyarchive.com